For Ros

with best wishes

Letters To My Grandchildren

A Life's Mosaic

from
Veronica

Veronica More

Pen Press

First published in Great Britain by Pen Press

All paper used in the printing of this book has been made from
wood grown in managed, sustainable forests.

ISBN13: 978-1-907172-15-1

Printed and bound in the UK
Pen Press is an imprint of Indepenpress Publishing Limited
25 Eastern Place
Brighton
BN2 1GJ

A catalogue record of this book is available from
the British Library

Cover design by Jacqueline Abromeit
Photographic research and editing by Cordelia Weedon

In loving memory of
my parents
Frank and Priscilla

Since children are the living corner-stone,
where marriage, built on both sides, meetes in one,
whil'st they survive our lifes shall have extent,
upon record in them our monument.

Inscription on 17th century parents' tomb,
Edington Church, Wiltshire.

Caminante son tus huellas
el camino, y nada mas;
Caminante, no hay camino,
se hace camino al andar.
Al andar se hace camino
y al volver la vista atràs
se ve la senda que nunca
se ha de volver a pisar.
Caminante no hay camino
sino estelas en la mar.

Antonio Machado 1875–1939

(Machado is telling us that in life there is no path to follow, we make
our own path as we go and when we look back and see the path we
have made we know we shall never have to tread it again. There is no
path only the wake in the sea.)

Dearest Olivia

This is to bring you a small cheque and lots of good wishes for your birthday. I get a bit muddled these days with birthdays but yours I never forget. November 23rd 1959 is a date printed indelibly on my mind. It was the day your grandfather died and my world, as I knew it, fell apart. When you were born twenty years later on that very same date I felt it as an especially joyful event that new life should replace loss of life. How fitting that one of Tom's grandchildren should be born on the date he died so soon after his own fifty-first birthday, on October 16th.

When I emerged from the house on the morning after he died, to go to the children, it seemed as if the oranges had ripened during the days of his dying. The winter sun was just topping the mountains as I left the village and below them the citrus harvest glowed bright against its dark green leaves, still safe from the encroaching car parks that future 'progress' would bring. The brightness of the scene made me blink. I felt like something that had crawled out from underneath a stone – drained, putty coloured and sere. I had forgotten that there was still beauty.

I was accompanied by your grandfather's brother Wilfred who had come to Fornalutx two days previously. No two brothers could have been more different than your grandfather and your great uncle Wilfred. Tom used to say he couldn't believe they had stemmed from the same womb. But they did have one thing in common – their love of opera. We drove towards Deià where your Dad and the other children had been staying with Beryl and Robert Graves for the past two or three days. My arrival at the house would not herald any unexpected news. Everyone knew that Tom was dying, my appearance was

1

just confirmation of his end. Your Dad was busy making a model boat with Tomàs Graves and Martin was shunting his toy car round the floor, making appropriate noises. They both redoubled their attention on what they were doing when I came into the room. Only Fiona burst into sobs and hid her face in my skirts. There was no sign of Cordelia, and Beryl said she had gone into the garden. I found her on the swing near Robert's famous compost heap, dragging her feet in the dust as she swung listlessly to and fro. When I asked her to come back to the house, wanting to draw her into some orbit of comfort, she shook her head and I left her swinging, inaccessible in her grief. Back indoors Tom Simon was crying quietly, Martin concentrated fiercely on his car and Fi sobbed noisily and clung for comfort.

Tom was to be buried that same evening which is the custom in Spain, at least in rural areas. The village priest had been a friend of his and together they had gone on an expedition photographing hilltop monasteries and Tom had made recordings of singing in the church. Your grandfather was the first foreigner to be buried within the precincts of the cemetery. I think it was his doctor, an influential citizen of Sóller, who had urged the priest – bury him first and ask the Bishop afterwards. It was quite a courageous thing to do because it was well before the days of ecumenism and Tom was not a practising Christian, let alone a Catholic. It could well have evoked strong disapproval from the ecclesiastical hierarchy.

I did not know what to do about the children. I wanted to protect them from the painful trappings of death and at the same time it was their right to attend their father's funeral if they so wished. Cordelia elected not to come, I think in the fantasy that if she wasn't present it hadn't happened. Both the boys said they would come. To Fiona I did not wish to give any choice. I wanted to keep her removed from the reality of death. I felt she was too young, too emotional to be exposed to such an experience and I was afraid for her of the terrors it might evoke seeing her father in his coffin. But I reckoned without her persistence. I had to return to Fornalutx to see to various things and Tom Simon and Martin were to be brought over later in the day. But Fiona would not let me go. She clung to my skirts crying for me to take her, crying to see her father.

Against my better judgement I took her with me. When we got back to the house, it had all been tidied up and Tom had been laid in his coffin. The pain and stress had flowed out of his face and he looked easily ten years younger. The furniture had been removed from the room and the coffin placed on a table tilted towards the window, the sunshine filtering through the shutters and making criss-cross patterns on the rough, white walls. People had brought plants and flowers which were placed on the table and on the floor. I remember thinking that Tom would have found it photogenic.

I lifted Fiona up so that she could see her father. She did not appear to pay much attention, she didn't say anything. There were other people in the room. They came and went at intervals throughout the day, just as they had come and gone throughout the days and nights of Tom's week long dying to support and help me. *"Pobrecita"* someone said as I put Fiona on the floor again. What had she understood? I did not know, but I remember that throughout her childhood she carried a profound fear of death. I was dropping with exhaustion and together she and I lay down in bed and, with the comfort of her warm little body in my arms, we both fell asleep.

That evening Fiona did not protest at going back to Deià in the car which had brought Robert Graves and the two boys for the funeral. There was no church ceremony. Six men carried the coffin, preceded by the priest and altar boys carrying the tall, lighted candles which Tom so often loved to photograph. It was a clear, moonlit night and the procession wound silently along the narrow road on the hillside which led to the cemetery. More people joined the procession as we progressed. In those days it was not tradition for the widow to go to the cemetery, she went back to her house after the Mass. But I was

3

not Spanish and clutching Tom Simon and Martin in either hand, I trudged behind Tom's coffin, seeing the candles ahead of us winking like glow-worms in the darkness. I remember noticing that Martin had a long dirty smudge on one cheek and Tom Simon had his shirt hanging half out of his shorts as usual, they had not been spruced up exactly for the funeral.

At the cemetery they laid the coffin in the tiny chapel and removed the lid for the mourners to file past. Then we went out into the graveyard again where the priest said a prayer for all the dead. Afterwards we returned to the house and people came to present their condolences to me. I remember it as a jumble of faces in the dim lit *entrada*. We then drove over the mountains in our van, back to Robert and Beryl's where we had supper and stayed the night. Wilfred went to the *fonda* in the village.

The next morning was brilliant and sunny. The children went off to pick olives with their friends and I sat on the terrace outside the house and let the sun soak in, hoping it would have some re-vitalising magic. I seemed to see, hear and feel everything through a cotton wool-like filter. Later in the morning I drove Wilfred to the airport for his return to London. And then I went back home again where I was to have one day on my own to prepare for the children's return. The final clearing up of the house had been completed. As per custom, the room in which Tom had died had been whitewashed. Our maid, Catalina, was still in the house. She made me a cup of coffee, asked if there was anything else she could do, then left with her usual *'hasta mañana'* – until tomorrow. Tomorrow and tomorrow and all the tomorrows that were to follow. What was I going to do with them? For the first time since Tom took ill I was alone in an empty echoing house with a life full of question marks before me and all sorts of decisions, large and small, to be made. It was important not to be overwhelmed by what lay ahead. One parent had crumbled away into the dust, the other must not crumble into chaos, confusion nor despair.

Well, Livvy, I suppose this is not really the sort of birthday letter you might be expecting but I'm not really being dismal. It was the meaningful date that took me back all those years. You may think it is irrelevant to your young life, and so in a way it is. But it is your family history and you are attached to it for better or worse.

Anyway, have a lovely day and lots of happy years to come.

My love to you,

    from your loving grandma
    Veronica

Dearest Thomas

Thank you for your letter, I'm glad you all had a good flight back. It was a great holiday and you were lucky with the weather. I can't think why I was so surprised when you said that you didn't know that I had ever worked and thought that I had always lived in Fornalutx. After all you were born just as I retired and you've never known me anywhere else. So if nobody told you, how could you know?!

But yes, I've lived in lots of other places but nowhere for so long as I have lived here. After your grandad Tom died in 1959 my family and friends in Britain all expected me to sell up and come home. I don't think the idea ever crossed my mind. It had been such an enormous upheaval moving out here and most of the organisation of the move had been my responsibility because Tom was hospitalised for many weeks before we moved. In fact he was expected to die but didn't. I think the prospect of Fornalutx was what kept him going and he survived the crisis and got 'well' again. He suffered from a condition known as nephritis, which is damage to the kidneys which was thought to have been caused by certain medication he had been given during his war service. Both his kidneys were affected. It was diagnosed about eight years before his death and at first it did not make much impact on his day-to-day life. Now and again he suffered terrible headaches accompanied by vomiting but the attacks did not last long and he soon recovered. He was a very positive man was your grandad and he was determined to pay as little attention as was humanly possible to his condition.

After the trauma of his death I did not want to move from the village and the house which had enfolded us both in a way it is difficult to describe. I thought we would be better off – all

7

of us – to remain where we were and try in our individual ways to come to terms with being fatherless and husbandless. I flirted very briefly with the idea of remaining permanently in Fornalutx and sending the children back to school in Britain. But I knew it was not on, not really. I was in my early forties and I knew I was too young to bury myself in this lovely backwater, despite strong unfulfilled urges to become a writer. We needed money, I would have to get a job and to do this I had to return to Britain. So eventually, after two and a half years, back we went to Newdigate in Surrey, to Cedar Cottage, our first home and where your father was born. No, I am wrong to say it was our first home, it was the first home we owned.

After the war, accommodation was hard to come by and also we did not really know where we wanted to live nor what we were going to do. At the time of our marriage in January 1946 (we were married at the Chelsea Register Office) we were renting a couple of rooms in a beautiful airy flat in Putney belonging to the Viennese photographer Lotte Meitner Graf, famous for her portraits of well-known people. But this was coming to an end, partly because the rent made too much of a hole in our meagre earnings – we were trying to sell articles and photographs to magazines and I was doing some freelance baby sitting, shopping etc. for handicapped people and other odd jobs which were available at the time. But also our landlady wanted to regain full possession of her flat.

So after we were married we moved into a pretty grotty room in a boarding house in the Bloomsbury area of London. There was a grim little kitchen off our room which took me ages to clean up. We shared a bathroom with some of the other lodgers. I got a job in an advertising firm near Piccadilly which earned me a fiver a week. This paid the rent leaving two pounds, ten shillings over (two pounds fifty p. to you). Your grandfather pursued his photography, making some money from photo journalism. His first big success was with *Picture Post* which published his series of photos of soldiers from the Seaforth Highlanders dancing highland flings and sword dances in the Colosseum in Rome (where we made an unauthorised visit the day after the Germans moved out) and also taking portraits of young children which he was very good at. The beastly little kitchen frequently doubled as a dark room. And so we scraped by. One day the legs of our bed broke and it was propped up on wooden blocks 'temporarily' – so it remained until we left.

We spent six months in London before embarking on our ill-fated journey through part of post-war Europe and into Spain in July 1946. When we returned to the UK in the autumn (myself by air direct to St. Thomas' Hospital in London and your grandad after a long, solitary journey in our unreliable van), we were homeless. The night Tom arrived in England he went to his parents' home in Iver, Buckinghamshire. His mother, your great-grandmother, Alice, was in hospital following a heart attack and she died that night without Tom ever seeing her again. It was very sad, she was 72. When I was discharged from hospital after about three weeks, I went home to my parents in Edinburgh to convalesce. Tom had no alternative but to stay on in Iver with his bereaved Dad and his brother Wilfred as he had found some part-time teaching at Epsom Art College.

After this enforced separation we finally found a flat in a wonderfully decayed mansion on the Hog's Back near Guildford, called Monk's Hatch. It had once been the home of the poet, Tennyson. There was sweeping oak staircase and an oak-panelled music room with composers' heads carved on the wooden panels, by then encrusted in dust and dirt from the chicken battery which provided the only music issuing from that room when we moved in. The then owner was a business man who lived rather grandly on the next-door estate and who used Monk's Hatch for purely agricultural purposes and, I suspect, tax relief. The house was surrounded by several acres of picturesquely neglected parkland and gardens. We found a badger's sett in the chalk cliff opposite the front of the house. The noise and the smell which came from the chicken battery

9

in the music room was disgusting but luckily it didn't percolate to our quarters which were on the first floor. We were amply compensated by having the most wonderful views across the Surrey countryside to Hindhead. On the floor above us, several landgirls were housed, so named during the war because they worked on the land.

Here it was that your aunt Cordelia spent the first year of her life, mostly in her pram in the overgrown rose garden. Her eyes were the colour of violets and she had a healthy pair of lungs which she used to good effect. From her father she inherited an enchanting smile which I think she has kept ever since. The death of your great-grandfather in the autumn of 1949 left Tom with a small inheritance and we were able to contemplate buying our own house. We would have to raise a mortgage as well as there was not a lot of money and what it would buy (or what others would regard as a 'sensible purchase') was some suburban semi-detached. This wasn't really our idea of a home and so we wasted a lot of time viewing 'barn for conversion'; 'stables semi-converted, planning permission promised'; 'delightful cottage in rural surroundings, in need of repair'. All of which required financial outlay way beyond our resources.

Then we saw Cedar Cottage, timber framed and the top half hung with cedar wood tiles. It stood in two and a half acres of wild woodland. It was within our price range and we had no hesitation. There were murmurings of concern from my side of the family and also possibly from Wilfred, about the unwisdom of investing money in a wooden framed house as opposed to one built of brick. But these prejudices were unfounded and Cedar Cottage maintained a market value on a par with all the more solidly built houses in the neighbourhood long after we had left it – admittedly with many improvements (brick built) and manicured grounds. But when we returned to Cedar Cottage from Fornalutx (it had been rented in the interim) I couldn't settle. It was not just the sadness of bygone memories and the flitting ghosts of the past, nor the depressingly

10

appalling state in which the tenants had left it, I just felt incapable of coping on my own with the land and the now and again blocked drains from the septic tank. Besides it was not a good base from which to try to find a job which was becoming increasingly necessary.

I put the house into some semblance of order, painting and papering into the small hours. Then I sold it (to friends) and bought a flat in London. I don't think your father ever forgave me (I hope he has by now!) but he loved Cedar Cottage and hated London.

So these are some of the places I have lived in, not forgetting of course, Edinburgh in my youth, wartime London, wartime Egypt and Italy. I'll tell you about them some other time. Have a good first term at College and see you at Christmas.

Lots of love,
    your loving g'ma
      Veronica

Dearest David

Your Mum told me the other day on the phone that you have got that post as a teacher that you applied for. Congratulations! Fancy you being a teacher when you so disliked school and were not infrequently in trouble. I expect this will make you a very good one and understanding of kids who don't want to learn.

When we lived in Fornalutx in the years following your grandfather's death, your dad and uncle and aunts had the misfortune to be taught by me, their mother! That was in the mornings and in the afternoons they went to the village schools. When the boys came home with dusty knees I knew they hadn't learnt their lesson properly. The boys' school was in a large rather gloomy room which contained all the village boys between the ages of seven and fourteen. There was one schoolmaster to teach them all. Learning was by rote. What they learned came from one school book called the *Enciclopedia*. This had religion at the front and ended in politics with a bit of general knowledge and rudimentary maths sandwiched in between. There were different volumes for different age groups. What mattered was that the boys could repeat their lesson word perfect, whether they understood it or not was immaterial. Those who did not know their lesson had to kneel on the concrete floor, facing the wall and relearn it. That was in the bad old days of Franco and they sang the Falangist song, *cara al sol*, at the end of each school day – something modern Spain does not wish to be reminded of.

Most of the girls, and boys under seven, went to the nuns' school but your aunts went to a so-called state school in the house of the schoolmistress. There were about eight pupils. Reading, copperplate writing, religion and embroidery were the main subjects. As you may well imagine I didn't really expect them to learn very much from their afternoon 'schooling'. The idea was that by attending the village schools in the afternoons they would be integrated with the village children and make friends, which they did. Their real schooling was with me, each morning at 9 a.m. sharp, after breakfast, in the small room at the top of the house which is now my upstairs kitchen. It was still referred to as the schoolroom long after it ceased to be one. I don't think it's a very good idea parents teaching their own children, do you? I wonder what would have happened if your parents had had to teach *you*?! We were not left with much alternative.

In the run-up to our move out to Mallorca, I made contact with an educational organization which provided syllabuses for home teaching. It was called the Parents' National Education Union or more briefly, known as the PNEU. They also had schools in Britain, I remember one in Edinburgh which I used to pass every morning on my way to school. The organization actually goes back to the Victorian era when it was formed to assist parents in the outposts of Empire to educate their children. I must say it was very efficient and I had a syllabus for each child every term. Like the Fornalutx teachers, I had to teach children of different ages but there the similarity ended. The PNEU was very keen on the use of books so there was quite a financial outlay on text books. Their philosophy of education was that a child is a seeker after knowledge and not a vessel to be filled, so there was no rote learning except tables and poetry. They had to do exams twice a year which were sent back to the PNEU headquarters in the UK for marking. The questions were angled to find out how much a pupil knew rather than how little.

It was difficult to separate my double role as parent and teacher and make the split meaningful to the children. For instance, to begin with I would call them each morning from upstairs when it was school time and they would appear in dribs and drabs, calling up to me: I'll be up soon – coming in a minute. It was Mum who was calling them from upstairs. This did not suit me and I pondered on a solution. The next time I was in Sóller I bought a sheep bell and this I rang when it was school time. It worked like a charm. The children scampered upstairs without quibbling. Mum didn't ring bells! I also used it to signify the end of a lesson. I always had to be one step ahead of my pupils, so this meant I had to do my homework in the evenings as well as correcting the day's written work. The only time I had to myself was the two hours in the afternoon when they were all at the village schools and I was blissfully alone. During that time I sorted and read old letters and diaries of your grandad's and mourned my loss.

The children acquired a puppy, a present from Beryl and Robert. He was a poodle and came from the same family as the Graves' poodles. We called him Tildy – a *tilde* is the squiggle over the Spanish 'n', used in certain words. Cordelia was his main owner and responsible for training him. He was a very highly strung and jealous animal and one morning I came downstairs and found he had bitten the heads off our tiny kittens. I had to move swiftly and clear up the massacre before the children came down to breakfast. Tildy had the grace to look very ashamed and slunk away behind the armchair. He also went missing in Palma, shot off from the cafe where we were sitting but we recovered him. He did not come to Britain with us, we left him with an American lady who was a violinist. But it wasn't a great success – he didn't like the violin! He finally ended up with a South American couple.

I would never have got by had it not been for Magdalena. She came to us shortly after Tom died. We originally had the services of one Apolonia who was a great character. She was quite old and more or less toothless and had a wonderful sense of humour but she had to give up work and she found us Catalina as a temporary measure. Catalina was employed by another family but they were away at the time. Magdalena was introduced to me by our builder. She was young and energetic and became my friend and adviser. She kept the domestic

15

wheels turning. She cooked and shopped and cleaned, arriving at 7.30 in the morning with a shovelful of glowing charcoal from her mother's fire to get ours going. But always, always I had to decide each morning what we were going to eat for that day. Before I left the breakfast table Magdalena would come to me and say, "Señora, what are we eating today?" I was never let off the hook by any suggestion on her part and sometimes when my mind was a complete blank I would appeal to the children.

I don't think I had the best temperament for a teacher. My patience was inclined to wear thin and I don't doubt you have heard the story of how I hurled the alarm clock at your father's head. Completely untrue! I banged it down on my desk and the glass which was very badly fitting fell out and shattered. But that doesn't make such a good story! I did throw the odd indiarubber and maybe pieces of blackboard chalk and – oh yes, to my shame – I broke the lid of his pencil box on your poor dad's head. In my defence I have to say it was made of *very thin* wood. Your dad and I fell out mainly over mental arithmetic and square roots. Fiona took a great dislike to history, admittedly the history book – *Our Island Story* – was pretty tedious, but anyway Fi just clapped her hands over her ears and refused to listen to anything so I was compelled to pick her up bodily and take her to her room where she had to stay until she became more reasonable. Mind you, I don't want you to think that the schoolroom was a battlefield, it was only now and again that things erupted, mostly it was friction-free and often quite fun. In January 1960, our second term, the daughter of a Newdigate neighbour came to help me with the schooling. She took over all the maths and some of the science subjects and this lightened my teaching burden.

After we returned to Britain the three eldest went to boarding schools, Tom and Martin to a PNEU prep school in Surrey and Cordelia to a PNEU school in Worthing. Fiona went to the Newdigate village school until I moved to London and then she went to a PNEU day school for a year in London, after which she went to a co-educational boarding school near Godalming. She was keen to go to a boarding school and it was me who wept when the school coach bore her away. But Cordelia was by now a weekly boarder and came home for the weekends so I was not entirely alone. In some ways, looking back, I feel as if I had made rather a dog's dinner of my children's secondary education. I was trapped between the norms of my parents' thinking on education on the one hand and not having enough money to pay for really good schools on the other. Having said that, Fiona went to a really good school but possibly not best suited to her needs and in her last year she grew to dislike it. Maybe I should have sent them all to state day schools. Who knows? And then how would I have managed my social work training? Anyway much water has run under many bridges since then and I don't think I inflicted any lasting damage.

I'm sure your experience of being a teacher is going to be very interesting and I hope you enjoy it.

Lots of love, and good luck

G'ma Veronica

Dearest Stephanie

I've been thinking about you all this week and wondering how you are getting on in faraway Boston. I hope the flight was OK and that you are beginning to settle down with your American family.

When I was your age, or a little younger, I spent nine months with a family in Germany, it must have been around 1936/37. From today's perspective and knowing what we now know, it could seem strange a strange choice. It was not my parents' decision but mine. They wanted to send me to a so-called finishing school or a family, in Switzerland or France. I didn't find this a very exciting prospect although a number of my friends would be doing exactly that. University was only for the brainy girls and I wasn't considered brainy, also I wasn't much interested in further academic learning.

LIFE was what beckoned at seventeen when I left school. My brother Francis had been to Oxford but that was expected of him as the boy in the family. My sister, Elizabeth had spent several months with an interesting family in Lausanne, with whom Francis had also stayed for some time prior to going to university. But I wanted to tread my own path and not follow in the footsteps of my elder siblings.

The previous summer I had been on holiday with my parents to Morocco on a German cargo boat. The captain of the boat, which was quite small, was a tall good-looking man from Hamburg and I rather fancied him although he must have been twenty years older than me, and married. But anyway, at seventeen I received my first kiss on the deck of a German cargo boat, under the Mediterranean stars. Possibly this had some bearing on my desire to go to Germany! Be that as it may, I had a cousin who was a journalist, Ian Colvin, the

19

youngest of my painter cousin, Anne's three elder brothers. Ian worked as a foreign correspondent for a newspaper called the *News Chronicle* and he was based in Berlin. My parents consulted him about any families he might know and he suggested a family he knew quite well, called von Varnbüler who lived in Stuttgart. Arrangements were made for me to go there. My uncle Tommy, the youngest of my father's brothers who worked at the War Office (as the present Ministry of Defence was then called) conveyed his strong disapproval to my parents of my going to Germany. He said it was not a good place to send me and potentially dangerous. But I airily dismissed his objections and prevailed upon my parents.

I was, of course, politically totally illiterate. Politics were seldom discussed in our family. I imagine my parents voted Conservative, although my mother had been before her marriage, an active, but not aggressive suffragette. Occasionally my father would get aerated about some political event, but I didn't pay much attention. As far as Fascism and Communism were concerned I veered more towards Fascism. I saw Communists as long-haired men who didn't wear ties and who wore sandals – non conformists in other words and I was pretty conformist in my younger years. To me the Fascists seemed more orderly, and neat and tidy in their uniforms. Some yardstick by which to make political judgements!

So, I was all set for my continental adventure (in my young days Europe was referred to as the Continent). I had never travelled by myself before and was excited by the prospect, and slightly apprehensive. I had to catch the *Orient Express* which left Calais at four in the afternoon. Details of the actual journey have not stayed with me, lost in the mists of time, but I probably travelled south from Edinburgh by night train and then made my way to the boat train at Victoria station. Once across the Channel I remember feeling I had really left Scotland behind me, there was a certain glamour surrounding the *Orient Express* which went all the way to Istanbul. It was the month of January and very cold and I was wearing what was then called a teddy bear coat and a green felt hat. When we steamed out of Calais station dusk was beginning to fall. My main luggage had been sent from Edinburgh 'luggage in advance', a service which I don't think the railways offer nowadays. It meant that I only had a small suitcase with me and didn't have to bother about the rest until I picked it up in Stuttgart.

I can remember being rather disappointed in the other passengers. I had expected them to be interesting and mysterious somehow but they were, in fact, mostly quite large parties of rather noisy Brits. I remember I had a very comfortable sleeping compartment for two but I was the only one in it. At the frontier, at Aachen, I was awakened by the train attendant to show my passport and fill in a form to say how much money I had on me, giving the numbers of my traveller's cheques. After that I woke at each station we stopped at and anxiously consulted my watch. We were due to arrive in Stuttgart at 5 a.m. and I was terrified that I would fall asleep and not wake up and be carried on to... Istanbul! Small danger of that. We arrived in what was then the big, domed cathedral like station of Stuttgart (it was bombed during the war and subsequently re-built) to a fanfare of noise, the clunking of the wheels as the train drew to a halt, shrill blasts on the engine's steam whistle and shouts from the platform. It had been arranged that I would carry a white handkerchief for recognition purposes but as I was almost the only passenger to get off the train my meeting up with Ursula, the younger daughter of the family, was not a problem.

The family consisted of the *Frau Baronin* who was very stout and motherly. She was a war widow from the first world war (her husband had been a colonel in the *Wehrmacht*) and she had two daughters, Beatrix, the elder, was quiet and I thought rather nice. In conversation she would help me with my language difficulties and was not impatient like Ursula who would immediately use English. Unfortunately I didn't see much of Beatrix as she worked as a secretary and left the house about eight and didn't come back until quite late. She was engaged to be married and spent most of her free time with her chap. Ursula, who was a year older than me, worked in the mornings in a nursery school. She was rather spoilt and attention seeking and had, I thought, considerably less charm than her sister. She went on endlessly about her boy friends, in fact didn't talk about much else and I got very fed up with her and delighted when I could go off independently. Having said that, we had a lot of fun together, long bicycle rides, walks and excursions. She was better out of the home than in it.

Home consisted of a top floor flat in a tall gabled house facing on to quite a wide thoroughfare sweeping up from the town centre – the *Rosenbergstrasse*. The flat was reached by a stone staircase or a rickety lift. It was wonderfully warm, there was a huge, tiled, wood fired stove in the sitting room which blazed like a furnace and seemed to heat the whole flat. I also had a small wood stove in my room which was lit on the colder evenings. My room was quite small and looked out onto the brick wall of the well of the building, so it was quite dark during the day. But after a month, I moved into a much larger room with a lovely sunny balcony. When I first arrived a sister of the *Baronin* was staying with them. I hardly saw her as she only appeared at mealtimes, spoke very little and then immediately after the meal disappeared to her room, so I only have a very hazy memory of her. But I was very pleased when she left and I inherited her room.

I had a ewer and basin in my room and at night was provided with hot water, but not in the morning. There was a little maid called Analiese who slept in the attic and pottered about the flat during the day and it was she who brought my hot water, lit my stove and made my bed.

It was then I had my first encounter with a duvet or *plumeau* as the Germans called it. But it was not like the duvets we know today. It was immense like a huge snow mountain, a vast envelope of goose feathers encased in a snow-white embroidered linen cover, none of your polyester, it hadn't been invented. In Edinburgh I slept with three blankets which were tucked in and an eiderdown, all rather heavy. I couldn't imagine that I would be warm enough beneath this frothy thing that didn't tuck in. How wrong I was! Baths were an event, a battle with the gas geyser. Also they were extra, one deutschmark per bath. I decided I could only afford two baths a week.

However strange you may be feeling, Steph, with your American family, at least you can understand what they are saying to you. My German was non-existent. I had done some desultory study with Linguaphone records but... the grandfather sits in his chair and smokes his pipe... or... the little dog barks... doesn't get one very far in everyday communication! Luckily Ursula spoke quite good school English and that was a great help in the early days. But then gradually, almost without noticing it, I realised I was beginning to understand more and more of what was being said. Mealtimes were no longer a jumble of incomprehensible sounds, I was learning to distinguish words and attach them to objects and slowly began to form rudimentary phrases.

I used to have my breakfast on my own about 9 a.m. – coffee and delicious black bread, butter and honey or sometimes an equally delicious pretzel. The daughters had already left for work and I don't think the *Baronin* got up for breakfast. I would try to talk with Analiese as she hovered around dusting and sweeping but she had a very strong Swabian accent so I could hardly understand anything she said.

At lunchtime there was usually Ursula and me and her mother. The *Frau Baronin* made a point of talking to me a lot at lunchtime and correcting what I said. She was a kindly woman and appeared very placid. I've no idea how old she was, to me at eighteen she just appeared 'old'. Probably in her mid fifties. She was massively large and wore shapeless dresses, her greying hair was swept up in a tight bun at the back of her head. She could have been the epitome of what used to be said about German women – the three Ks – *Kinder,*

Küche und Kirchen – (children, kitchen and church). Not that church was particularly evident. I only went once with them to church and that was to a wedding.

At suppertime usually the whole family was present with sometimes Beatrix's fiancé as well whom Ursula and I called Teddy because he was plump and cuddly. And occasionally some other relative was present as well. In the evenings I had to pay a great deal of attention in order to understand (some) of what was being said, they did not make any particular concessions to my lack of fluency during the evening meal.

You, Steph, have to earn your keep looking after the children in your American family. My keep was paid for by my father, plus he gave me a modest monthly allowance. The object of my stay in Stuttgart was to learn German, so I soon set about organizing lessons. The *Baronin* had a younger sister who lived not far away and I arranged to have daily lessons from her. She was called Margareta and was the most charming, cultured person. She was everything the *Baronin* wasn't – slim, tall and elegant. I used to wrap up well and set off after breakfast on those cold, frosty mornings to walk the twenty minutes to her flat. The drudgery of grammar teaching was not really up her street although we dutifully did just that for the first half hour or so. German grammar was a maze in which I frequently got lost. But I did my homework and slowly it seemed less difficult. But what Margareta really enjoyed was introducing me to German literature and poetry which made up the second half of my lessons.

I learned reams of German poetry by heart and this gave me the feel of the rhythm and beauty of the German language which can also sound so harsh and ugly. I have, of course, forgotten them all. No, not quite all. One poem has remained with me all my life. It is by the Swabian poet, Eduard Möreke and it tells of a young servant girl who has to get up at cock's crow, before the stars have faded from the sky, to kindle a fire on the hearth. The line... *Ich muss am Herde stehen/ Muss feuer zünden...* comes into my head every time I light a fire.

It's odd that it should have remained with me, I suppose because it is connected to an activity that has been quite constant in my life. Not that I am up before cock's crow and the stars are well gone when I light my fires!

Sadly, after two months my lessons with Margareta came to an end. She went away. I can't remember why she went away nor where she went to. But away she went and I transferred my lessons to the Berlitz School of Languages. There I was taught by a lovely old gentleman who looked as if he belonged to the nineteenth century. He was called Herr von Seydlitz, wore pin striped trousers, a tail coat, a black bow tie and spats (which in case you don't know are like short gaiters which cover the top of the shoe and are strapped round the ankle). My dad also wore them in the winter and they help to keep the shoe clean and the ankles warm. At the beginning of each lesson Herr Von Seydlitz clicked his heels and bowed and likewise at the end. He was a very good teacher and got down to much more basic stuff than ever I did with Margareta. No fancy poetry learning but the nuts and bolts of grammar and construction which he managed to make not boring and I learned a great deal more from him, I think, than ever I did from Margareta, but I had to work harder!

So what did I do apart from going to classes during my stay in Nazi Germany? I suppose I wasn't particularly conscious of the fact that I was living in 'Nazi Germany' as we came to think of Germany in the thirties and forties. The streets were full of uniforms – green uniforms, blue uniforms, black uniforms, brown uniforms – every organization, be it military or semi civil, seemed to have a uniform. At the time this did not present itself as anything particularly sinister, it just seemed very foreign and different from Britain. I never witnessed any unpleasant incident or violence concerning the German Jewish population during the whole of my stay there. But what I do remember were neat little printed notices hung on the doors or in the windows of most restaurants and cafes which stated – *Juden unerwünscht,* Jews not wanted. This struck me as offensive but I didn't detect the true menace behind it. When I mentioned it to Ursula, she just shrugged and said – "I suppose they go elsewhere." After all in Britain before the war, certain clubs, mostly golf clubs or tennis clubs refused membership to Jews. And what about my select primary school which excluded children of 'the trade' as it was called. This meant that the children of the owners of the oldest and most prestigious department store in Edinburgh, were not acceptable. Admittedly all this changed soon after I went there and it became more all embracing. But inclusion and exclusion were not entirely unknown concepts to me.

Sometime in early March, I think it was, we went skiing. This was my first and only experience of this sport. The *Baronin* would not let me go until she had received written permission from my father. We went to an area in Bavaria called the Allgaü which is a mountainous region between Germany and Austria. Where we were staying was hilly rather than mountainous with very suitable gentle slopes for beginners like me. We were joined by a schoolfriend of mine who was with a family in Munich, and a friend of Ursula's, so we were four. We all left Stuttgart in a ski train which was cramped and noisy and supremely uncomfortable with hard wooden seats. But the company was jolly and someone in our carriage had an accordion so there were bursts of spontaneous singing. We had brought bread, and sausages and oranges for the journey and so it seemed had everyone else. Very soon we started to eat and the whole carriage stank of *wurst* and oranges.

The journey took about four and a half hours and when we arrived there was a bus to take us on the next stage of our journey. The bus was even more crammed than the train. Our skis went on the roof and our rucksacks came with us inside the bus. The windows all steamed up as it was so hot inside and so cold outside. The bus ride took about an hour over a very bumpy road which towards the end of the journey became snow packed. By now it was dark and even if one could have seen out of the window it would have been difficult to get any idea of our surroundings. When we arrived at our destination, the farmer in whose house we were to lodge, met us with a hand sleigh to transport the luggage. Most people got on their skis and disappeared into the night.

As I had never been on skis in my life, I didn't think it was a good idea to start in the dark and so I plodded behind the farmer. Peggy, my friend, was an experienced skier, but the fastenings on one of her skis had broken so she walked with me. It was a moonlit night and we walked for just over half an hour under the stars, through thick snow which sometimes came up to our calves. Eventually we arrived at the little hamlet where we were staying, exhausted, damp and hungry. But we soon warmed up in the cosy farm kitchen where the farmer's wife plied us with thick slices of rye bread and cheese and mugs of hot tea.

We spent a very happy and healthy week in this snowbound little village. The farmhouse was primitive, but scrupulously clean. We washed in the shed next to the munching, moo-ing cows and there was a deep, dark earth closet for our other hygienic requirements. We were well fed with rather repetitive meals and both the farmer and his wife were kind and friendly as were their four enchanting children. I practised my skiing on the gentle slopes behind the village and at first fell about all over the place. But gradually I got my ski legs and started to improve and enjoy myself. The others went higher up the mountains but I stayed on the lower slopes with the other beginners who were mainly children being instructed by their parents. In one of the other houses there were four youths said to be champion skiers for the Hitler Youth. They built several jumps and performed complicated acrobatics. One of them kindly came to my aid when I was floundering about and for a couple of days gave me some helpful instruction, but then they left.

As we were practically on the Austrian border, Peggy and I thought it would be fun to go there. So we skied into Austria (it was mostly fairly flat) and spent the day there. This was before the *Anschluss,* when Hitler annexed Austria. Ursula and her friend couldn't come because they had no passports and anyway Germans were not allowed to travel outside Germany unless they could produce a really good reason, such as business, in order to obtain permission and passports.

At the end of the week we all separated, Peggy went back to Munich and Ursula and I returned to the flat in the *Rosenbergstrasse,* rather grubby and in need of baths, but supremely healthy. It had been a great week and very inexpensive but it was the first and last contact in my life with skiing. The war came, and afterwards there was not much money so skiing had become an elitist sport which only the well off could indulge in. But in the fifties your grandfather went to Switzerland with one of his photography evening students, Peter, with whom we had shared part of a summer holiday on Lake Lucerne. Peter was a regular and keen ski-er and so Tom also had a one-off skiing holiday but it was a great deal more rigorous than mine and he didn't enjoy it that much. Naturally I couldn't go as I had the little ones to look after.

I found Stuttgart an attractive town built up gently sloping wooded hills, like a basin really with the centre of the town at the bottom, its huge main station a distinctive feature and seemingly a general meeting point. I don't suppose I would be able to recognise Stuttgart today, it was severely bombed and subsequently rebuilt. I went for many a long walk through the woods, both by myself and with Ursula. There were also open air swimming pools in the woods and sometimes we went swimming, Ursula swam a bit better than me but not much.

When I think about it, a great deal of my time, when I wasn't studying, was taken up by walking and cycling. When spring and the better weather came round, Ursula and I went off for several days cycling. We took a train part of the way and then went cycling round the shore of Lake Constance which has one shore in Germany and the opposite one in Switzerland. In Germany it was known as the *Bodensee,* and

28

probably still is. We had a high old time, the weather was wonderful and we stayed in hostels. We cycled many kilometres and suffered several of the usual cycling mishaps – the odd puncture, a chain which flew off, skids and falls going too fast over potholes but nothing than could not be put right and no serious injuries. We even dared to try the water in the lake although it was still only May, but our dip was very brief.

Maybe this is the moment to tell you that during my stay in Nazi Germany, I fell in love for the first time. I'm happy to say it was not with a black-uniformed SS man nor with a brown-shirted *Gauleiter*, but with a junior army officer. The Varnbülers had strong military connections as Ursula's father and several of her uncles had been in the Kaiser's army. We were sometimes invited to military balls. These were somewhat formal affairs, very different from the dances I used to go to in the Assembly Rooms in Edinburgh or in people's private houses. It made a change, instead of dancing eightsome reels with spotty youths in kilts, I danced waltzes with slightly older young men in field grey uniforms. At the time I was unaware that these spotty youths in kilts would soon be off to war, many of them never to return, likewise the young men in field grey.

These military balls or dances followed a fairly strict protocol. On arrival, it seemed chaotic as everyone was searching for their partner. Each female guest was allotted an officer who would be what was called their *Tischherr* for the evening, *Tischherr* meaning literally Tableman. He sat next to her at supper and his role was to look after her from start to finish. I imagine the organisation of this was determined by rank on one side and social importance on the other. Anyway whoever you were paired off with you were stuck with for the rest of the evening and if he was a crashing bore – hard luck! After the initial confusion, once everyone had found their partners (there was a list on the notice board) we processed into supper, led by the Colonel and his lady, to the strains of music from the military band. After supper the dancing started. You danced with whoever asked you but at the end of each dance you were returned to your *Tischherr* accompanied by suitable bows and heel clickings. Very different from Edinburgh where you had a dance programme, hopefully filled up in advance with partners, but when you had none (and I never had a full programme) you either leaned against the wall, watching (hence the term wallflower) or you retired to the ladies to powder your nose and to be less conspicuous.

It was at one of these military do's that I met Albert. He was my *Tischherr*. We got on well and he was a very good dancer and I can remember not being that pleased when asked to dance by others and anxious to get back to my Tischherr. Afterwards we saw each other on a fairly regular basis, meeting under the clock in the *Hauptbahnhof* at about 8 in the evenings. Sometimes we went to cafes and at other times we walked across the park to his quarters in the barracks which was on the other side of the town from where I lived. He made coffee and we drank wine.

Once we went on an afternoon excursion to a castle some kilometres away from Stuttgart with one or two of Albert's friends. The company was agreeable apart from one person. Accompanying us was someone Albert told me was quite important in the Party, he was apparently the uncle of one of the other officers. I found him objectionable, conceited and self-important and I observed how the younger men deferred to him and laughed at his stupid jokes. When we were parting he invited me to meet him for a drink the following week and named the cafe. I was not as skilled then at getting out of unwanted social engagements as I subsequently became, and weakly accepted. When the day came I worried all the time until the evening and then just decided not to go. I later discovered that this man subsequently became the inhumane governor of a defeated Poland. So although my political intellect was not particularly sharp then, my instincts were.

It was, on the whole, a fairly innocent friendship, certainly by today's standards but the *Baronin* was not impressed. Albert should have come to the flat to pick me up and been given the once-over by her. I told Albert this and he laughed and said next time he would come to the flat. I remember there was a gap of about two weeks and I thought I had lost him, but then he phoned and arranged to pick me up the following evening. He turned up very smart and trim in his uniform and duly clicked his heels and kissed the *Baronin's* hand. He was from a very different social background to the Varnbülers, his father being a Lutheran minister. Anyway he seemed to pass muster with the *Frau Baronin* and we soon escaped. He was some eight years older than me.

If Margareta had introduced me to German poetry, Albert introduced me to German philosophers, principally Nietzsche – all rather above my head really. On his desk in his room was a photograph of a pretty girl with a tennis racquet. When I asked him who she was he told me it was the girl he was going to marry. She lived in the ill-fated city of Dresden which was flattened by British carpet bombing. She was a formidable tennis player who beat him at every game. They were not formally engaged but he told me he had given her his word and that he would never break it even if he knew he was going into a marriage that would not make him happy. This seemed to me daft, and it was my first encounter with what seemed to be a Teutonic obsession with honour and duty. This was the time of Edward VIIIth's abdication and all the furore about Mrs Simpson, and I was always being asked what I thought about it. Almost without exception the Germans said that he owed a duty to his country which outweighed his personal happiness and that he should give her up.

As it happened I heard from Albert after the war. He was living with his wife and two children in the cellar of their destroyed house in Dresden – two cookpots and few bits of crockery, all that was left of their possessions. He sent me an article he had written on Europe's post-war future and asked me if I could translate it into English and try to get it published. I managed to translate it but was unsuccessful in finding any periodical who would publish it. For obvious reasons our contact petered out. But several years later I saw his name in the *Sunday Observer* in connection with some NATO conference and he appeared to be a colonel in the new German army.

I went with Ursula to Berlin. We stayed with her rich relations who had a large house on the Wannsee lake, many servants and a Mercedes in the drive. Their two small boys always seemed to be in Hitler Youth uniform. I imagine they toed the Party line as much from expediency as from conviction. However it was very pleasant going out on the assorted boats that bobbed around the landing stage at the bottom of their lovely garden. But I was a pain to Ursula, I had just met Albert and was lovesick and didn't want to do anything except row dreamily round the lake. She got very irritated with me but I was in the throes of being in love for the first time and nothing else seemed to matter.

But I met and became pally with a friend of one of Ursula's older cousins. He was a very funny chap with a great sense of humour and a zippy little sports car in which we buzzed around as we went about our frivolous pursuits – picnics, tè dansants etc. etc. I was never the least bit attracted to him but I liked him as a person. It was he who said to me that marriage was a killer of romance – imagine, he said, a wife having to wake up every morning and watch her husband get into his underpants. I tried to persuade him that there were other aspects of marriage but he would have none of it. We corresponded after I went back to Scotland and in fact I heard from him after the war had been in progress for several months. He was in Rumania. I had no idea what he was doing there, I suspect trying to delay his call-up for as long as possible. He would have made an indifferent soldier. I never heard from him again and I sometimes wondered what had happened to him.

After a week Ursula went back to Stuttgart and I went to stay with my cousin, Ian Colvin, in his flat near the *Tiergarten*. He moved in rather different circles from me, journalistic, diplomatic, and he had several Jewish friends. He took me to visit a couple he was very fond of. The husband was a university professor but banned from his post and his wife was a journalist. I learned that it was not only in the cafes that *Juden* were *unerwünscht*. Ian was trying to help them get out of Germany. His view of the future was extremely pessimistic. He had grown up a lot since he stayed with the Varnbülers when, so the *Baronin* told me, he would drop stink bombs from his balcony at the feet of passers-by on the *Rosenbergstrasse* beneath, and he never had two *pfennigs* to rub together. But they were all very fond of him – "your mad cousin" they used to say to me. In a few days I was back on the train travelling south, happily wrapped in the solipsism of my untutored youth, expectant of another meeting with Albert. The young of today are far more aware of the world around them than some of us were in my day.

In August my parents came to Stuttgart and stayed for a few days in an hotel, coming to the flat to meet my German family. Then I went off with them to Pertisau in Austria where we were joined by Francis and Elizabeth for a family holiday on the shores of the lake. I think it was probably the last holiday we all had together and we had a lovely time, the scenery was magnificent and the weather perfect. We swam and walked and slept and ate (the food was good). Then Elizabeth and myself and two of her old school friends who had joined us for the last few days, walked over the mountains to Mittenwald in Bavaria where our parents and Francis had gone by train. It was my first experience of real mountain walking and I can remember the heat and the effort and the sweat dripping off my forehead and spotting the stones under my feet. It was quite a well defined path but steep and stony, a forerunner of the mule paths of the Mallorcan mountains which were to enter my life much later on. We spent the night in a refuge at the top of the pass and then set off the next morning downhill to Mittenwald where we arrived about lunch time. After a few days there we all dispersed and I went back to Stuttgart until the end of November.

And that, dear Steph, is the story of my sojourn in Stuttgart, so very different from what you must now be experiencing in Boston. Send me a card when you have a moment and let me know what you are doing.

Lots of love as always
your loving g'ma

Veronica

Dearest Alex

My youngest (very much my youngest) grandchild – all the others are now adults and some parents in their own right. But you are still a child and thinking of you makes me think back across all those years to my own childhood. What a different life, what a different sort of upbringing! But I think we would share at least one factor, that sense of discovery which is such an essential part of childhood, indeed of life, but in adults it becomes blunted by responsibilities and demands though hopefully it is never quite lost.

I spent the first eleven years of my life in a commodious four-storied (five if you count the basement) house in a sunny crescent on the north side of Edinburgh. I remember it as having long, long stairs on which were dark, rather spooky corners which I peopled with hobgoblins of my imagination. I was my parents' youngest child by five years. Francis and Elizabeth had only two years between them and the age gap, particularly between Francis and myself (seven years) often made me feel like an only child during the early part of my childhood when our respective daily timetables were so different and separate. My arrival was a grave disappointment to my brother and I think he may have resented the fact, for quite some time, of having another sister when he so desperately longed for a brother.

I was a so-called 'peace' baby, having been born on March 15th, 1919. My mother nearly coughed me into the world before my time as she had Spanish flu – that killer epidemic which carried off more lives than all the casualties of the war. I presume she did not have it very badly and we both survived. My father first fell in love with my mother from afar. He noticed her in the audience at the winter orchestral concerts in the Usher Hall and although he managed to get near her in the intervals, there was no question of him approaching her, he didn't even know her name. But he ferreted away among his friends and acquaintances and in the Edinburgh of those days it was not too difficult to find out who was who. Eventually an introduction took place and they did not look back from then on. They met in early March, became engaged at the end of April and married in October. Throughout their engagement they wrote to each other nearly every day, as well as meeting. My mother's father remarked, with a certain asperity, that he had never known an engaged couple meet so frequently! Shortly before they were married my grandfather became very unwell and as the reception was going to be in my mother's home they thought it would be all too much for him and they cancelled it. There was just the church service and then they went off to France for their honeymoon. My grandfather died a year later.

I was actually born in the same house as were my siblings, in Murrayfield, near the zoo. When I was a year old we moved to 4 Royal Circus which had belonged to my father's parents and, since his father's death, had been occupied by Granny More and Aunt Totty, my father's unmarried sister. It was far too large for them and they moved to a top floor flat in Grosvenor Street.

My father's forebears – the Mores – came from Fife. My great-great-grandfather, Francis More, was a weaver. Apparently three of his grandsons went to Australia and were involved in the Australian Gold Rush at Ballerat in Victoria. The fourth grandson, my grandfather, so the story goes, in order to better himself, walked barefoot to Edinburgh where he got himself a job as a clerk in an accountancy firm. He was an intelligent man, was rapidly promoted and became a partner with the result that in later years, his son (my father) became a partner in the same firm – Lindsay, Jamieson and Haldane – as did his son (my brother). The firm no longer exists, having been swallowed up by conglomerates. I remember being told as a little girl that my Daddy went to the office to make pennies and I had this vision of my papa busy at some infernal machine churning out pennies.

My father was born in Edinburgh in 1879. He had two elder sisters, Janey and Jessie (who was always known as Totty) and later his three younger brothers – John, Hugh and Tommy. As the eldest son he was named Francis, as his father before him and his grandfather before that, but he was always known as Frank. I don't know anything really about my grandfather More who died many years before I was born, but from snippets my mother (not my father) told me, I gathered that he was a very stern man. When, as a little boy, my father had cried for his mother to come and kiss him goodnight, his father beat him, not because he was a brutal man but because he believed boys shouldn't cry. Granny More was a gentle soul with a round, unlined face. She was always dressed from head to toe in black and I remember she wore a bonnet tied under her chin with black ribbons. She was entirely dominated by her bossy daughter, Totty, as she must have been by her stern husband. Curiously enough she bore no marks of life on her sweet, round face, no evidence that she had given birth to and reared six children. She suffered from asthma and had something called a tucker which she used to squirt some solution down her throat to ease her breathing problems. I have memories of Totty saying to her repeatedly – "use your tucker, mama, use your tucker." I believe she gave Granny breakfast in bed on a newspaper which horrified my mama who would never have given anybody breakfast in bed on a newspaper!

My mother's forebears – the Robsons – so far as we know came from the Border country. Her great-great-grandfather was a shepherd in Roxboroughshire. He moved his family to Kelso to take advantage of the school there and especially for one son who was disabled for a life of physical activity on account of an ankle injury at the age of ten. This son, John Robson, became a schoolmaster and was ordained in 1796. He married the daughter of a Berwickshire farmer and they had six children of which only one survived to marry and raise a family. Subsequently the Robsons branched out into the professions, they became doctors, lawyers, schoolmasters, some of them went to India and many of them went into the church – the Scottish Presbyterian church. My grandfather was a Minister of the Kirk and my mother was born in Inverness in January 1886, in a house called Netherwood. Her mother died five months after she was born, I think from stomach cancer. Thus my poor grandfather became a widower at the age of 46, with a family of seven, ranging from 17 years to 5 months, to care for.

My mother had four elder sisters and twin brothers. I imagine in her early years she was raised by her elder siblings and presumably a nursemaid. Then my grandfather remarried and the family moved to Perth where they lived in a house called Garry Lodge on the banks of the Tay between the two bridges. As adults, Elizabeth and I tried to locate where it might have been and decided that it had been pulled down to make way for modern flats. There were no children from this second marriage and when my grandfather married Catherine Young, he also had to offer the shelter of his house to her unmarried sister, Jessie.

I knew Granny Robson in her widowhood, by which time she lived in a pretty, small terraced house in Edinburgh. As a little girl I was taken to tea there by my Mummy. I remember Granny Robson as being a delicate little old lady with very fine bones and a mass of snowy-white hair piled high on her head. She wore a long black silk dress with a high neck edged in white lace. Great Aunt Jessie was still alive, she was a much larger, plainer woman who didn't say much. A maid would bring in the tea tray and then the cake stand and I would watch this diminutive person pour out our tea (I think I had milk) into fine bone china cups. I used to sit on a leather pouffe and be on my best behaviour, speaking when spoken to and not making crumbs. It was very boring, especially all the grown-up talk, but worth it for the finely cut cucumber sandwiches and yummy cakes! Then sometimes Granny got out the tiddly winks and I was allowed to get on the floor and play with them, flipping them into the wooden cup.

My mother was fond of her stepmother and when she was in India in her early twenties, staying with the surviving twin brother, Bobby, who was a doctor, she wrote both her parents long and affectionate letters. Bobby was a missionary doctor and worked for several years in India. His twin brother John had died of appendicitis in his early thirties, a year after his marriage. Bobby himself died prematurely, run over by a London bus when he was cycling round to see his patients in the practice he set up in London on his return from India. He used to visit us sometimes in Edinburgh with his Swiss wife Helène and he was one of my favourite uncles. My mother loved him dearly and when she came to tell me of his death it was the first time I had seen a grown-up cry.

I saw a lot more of Granny More than I did Granny Robson, because she and Totty often came to Sunday lunch and we would go back to their flat for tea, and they always came to Christmas dinner. I don't think Granny Robson ever visited us. But Totty dominates my memory of those visits. She had a lively personality and must have been vivacious and good looking when young. She and Hugh were the only members of the family not to have married and when Hugh retired (he was a doctor who spent much of his life in India, mainly as the doctor of the Madras to Bombay railway company) he and Totty lived together in the flat in Grosvenor Street. Totty died first and Hugh lived there on his own until well into his eighties, lunching at his club and having someone come in to cook his supper. Totty could be good company, but she could also be quite nasty and I think she was very jealous of my mother and didn't spare her criticisms. "That child should never be allowed to speak to her brother like that." Me of course, being cheeky to Francis, our probable ages, ten and seventeen.

Royal Circus was a big house but without many rooms on each floor. On the ground floor there was an outer and inner hall, divided by glass doors. On the left there was the smoking room where coal fire was lit in the mornings. It was a cosy sort of room, less formal than the drawing room which was on the next floor up. It was where the telephone, when we eventually got one, was installed and also it was where the crystal wireless set which Francis made at school, sat on a table on one side of the fireplace and I remember listening most evenings to Children's Hour through earphones and the reception was remarkably good. I listened to rather different material through earphones in my later years.

Next to the smoking room was a large, rather gloomy dining room which housed a substantial sized organ at one end. My father used to play it occasionally and when I was old enough I loved pumping the bellows. On the opposite side of the hall from the dining room were stairs, hidden by a glass partition, leading down to the basement. Halfway down there was a walk-in cupboard which my mother kept locked. It had a very low ceiling and you had to bend your head when you went in. It was full of bags of flour, rice, lentils, barley, split peas, pots of jam and marmalade – all kinds of dried groceries and a few tins. I particularly remember there was a huge crock of preserved eggs, laid down in the summer and presumably used in the winter. Whenever the cook required more supplies they were doled out from the store cupboard. The store cupboard was kept topped up by purchases from Mr Buchanan, the grocer, who had a lovely shop down Stockbridge.

Stockbridge was a district just round the corner from Royal Circus, quite a steep hill running down to the Waters of Leith. Where 'rough' people lived, I was told, and I usually only went down there in the company of an adult. Certainly many of the houses were shabby and in bad repair. There was a man who was a drummer who lived not far down Stockbridge. Both he and his wife were alcoholics and he used to beat her up but when any neighbour or member of the public tried to intervene, the wife immediately attacked her would-be rescuer. But he was a magnificent drummer and performed very well twirling his drum sticks with great panache. They lived in a very insalubrious basement, pointed out to me once by Bella, my nanny. They had a little dog with a ruff round its neck and when they were sober, all three would sally forth, the man in the lead playing his drum, I think he also had a mouth organ fixed high up on his chest so that he could play it without using his hands. They would make a stand somewhere and a small crowd gathered, the wife going round with a cloth cap to collect the coppers. Sometimes they went quite far afield and even made it to Princes Street. I was never allowed to linger at any of these performances, but was chivvied on by whoever I was with, so I only heard them *en passant*, as it were.

But to return to Mr Buchanan, his shop was dark and full of big sacks containing flour and oatmeal and the shop smelled of mysterious spices. He himself was a tall, nice looking man with white hair and blue, blue eyes. He wore a dun-coloured storeman's coat over his clothes. He was soft spoken and always very kind to me. When he had taken my mother's order (goods were delivered by a boy on a bicycle) I would end up with a couple of dried apricots or a fistful of raisins which he gave me and which I immediately jammed into my mouth. Not so the sisters who ran the fruit and vegetable shop, they were fast and sharp and obviously had no time for children. I was always made to feel in the way, which I probably was, but not a grape nor a cherry did I ever get. Then there was Mr Meek, the butcher – large and formidable in his striped apron behind the huge block of solid wood which was his counter. And all those fearsome knives! At Sunday lunch, Totty would nearly always ask – "is this Meek's beef, Priscilla?"

The fish shop was what really intrigued me – the way they slapped the fish down on the marble slab. I thought I would like to have a fish shop one day, I may say it was a short-lived ambition!

But to go back to Royal Circus, there was a huge kitchen in the basement with big dressers round the walls and a large deal table, scrubbed almost white, in the middle of the room. The cooking was done on a coal fired range and there always seemed to be something simmering away on it. There was no electricity in the basement, only gas mantles, but once they were all lit they gave out a soft attractive light. The kitchen was at the back of the house and looked out on the backs of other houses and drying greens. The greens were narrow walled strips of earth sprouting straggly grass and furnished with poles to take the washing lines. To get there you had to go down a pitch dark stone stair of 14 steps, leading to the laundry and wine cellar. It was illuminated neither by gas nor electricity, and when my father went down to get the wine he took a torch, and when Mrs Henderson, who did the laundry went down, she took a candle. I found it more exciting to go down in the dark reciting to myself – "1 2 3 4 5 6 7, all good children go to heaven", and on 'heaven' I knew I was down.

I have a very clear memory of Mrs Henderson. She was like someone out of *My Fair Lady*. Quite slim and small, she wore a long black skirt and a white blouse with a high collar. When she went out she put on a long, grey coat and perched on her head a shallow, round, black straw hat with artificial flowers at the front. In the laundry she was enveloped in a large rubber apron. Mrs Henderson was a widow and she lived down Stockbridge in a very old tenement building facing the Waters of Leith, with her grown-up son. I remember when her son was killed in an accident, my mother coming back from visiting her was deeply shocked at the conditions in which she lived. Petite though she was, she must have been very strong to fill the boiler with pails of water from the washtub taps and then light a fire under it. In this the sheets were boiled and Mrs Henderson stirred them with a long pole. I liked to see it steaming and once I asked her if I could have a stir. "No, hen," she replied, "you're too wee." There was a big wringer through which the sheets (folded) were put several times before being hung out on the drying green. When she came another day to do the ironing, there was a flat table covered in a blanket and a piece of sheeting and the two very heavy irons were heated alternately on a sort of brazier contraption.

At the front of the basement was the maids' bedroom, a long narrow room looking out on the area where the coal sheds were and from where you went up stone steps to the street, what used to be called the Tradesmens' Entrance. We had a cook and a house tablemaid (who the English call a parlour maid) and a nanny. I don't really remember any of them properly until Bella arrived, apart from one cook called Lizzy. She had bobbed red hair and used very white face powder, and I wondered whether it might be flour, her lips were a dazzling red. But I remember her mainly because she left us and went to America from where she sent back postcards and once, silk stockings (the forerunners of nylons). My mother used to go down to the kitchen every morning after breakfast to 'give the orders'. In other words to discuss the food for the day with the cook and write the menus down on a small slate. She had problems thinking about puddings and we had a lot of chocolate cornflour.

Having explored the basement, we better go upstairs again. On the first floor were the drawing room and our parents' bedroom with a bathroom/dressing room off it. The drawing room was a long elegant room with two tall windows which reached almost from the floor to the ceiling. It had an Adam's style fireplace and accommodated a Blúthner grand piano which both my parents played, my father by ear and my mother from music scores and on which, when I was old enough, I had piano lessons. The fire was usually lit in the afternoon and my parents sat there after dinner in the evening. After I had had my tea in the nursery, I used to go downstairs to the drawing room and there I would be read to by my mother, and we would play games until my bedtime. I enjoyed that, but what I did not enjoy was having to appear at her tea parties. I was scrubbed up by my nanny after having my tea and put into a clean dress and sent down to the drawing room. I used to hover for several minutes outside the closed door before I could pluck up the courage to go in and face this group of old women (they must have been all of 35 to 40) on my own, my mother always appeared ageless to me. This hang-up of my childhood has pursued me into adult life, I often feel apprehensive when faced with a social gathering. But finally I would reach up, turn the door handle and go in. There they all were (perhaps 4 or 5 persons) at the far end of the room, sitting round a blazing fire, sipping their tea, eating wafer-thin slices of bread and butter and Macvitties or Mackay's cakes and I think all the visitors wore hats. My shyness abated somewhat when I joined them and perched on a vacant chair. I wasn't offered anything off the tea table, I had already consumed much thicker slices of bread and butter and jam and a piece of home-made gingerbread cake upstairs in the nursery. They asked me kindly questions about what I had been doing that day and I remember once being asked what I was going to do when I became a 'big girl'. I replied without hesitation – "a writer of course." I must then have been writing my 'Storeys for Bos and Gels'. When the visitors made moves to leave, I would sometimes say to them – "Buster will take you home in the Rolls." They would look at my mother, slightly bewildered and she would laugh and say – "Oh, Buster is an imaginary friend of Veronica's." I obviously had delusions of grandeur!

Throughout my early childhood I had quite a cast of imaginary friends who I played with and with whom I had (to me) very real conversations. Later on, when I was older and had what would be considered as 'real' friends, I still had a very active imagination. Before I learned to read, my mother read to me. *The Wind in the Willows*, the A.A. Milne *Pooh* books, *Alice in Wonderland*, Mrs Molesworth, Stevenson's *A Child's Garden of Verses* etc. etc. Well, that was all very fine but once I could read for myself, I branched out into adventure stories, *Coral Island*, *Treasure Island*, the Fenimore Cooper books and sometimes I would transform my nursery (probably

44

upgraded to a playroom by now) into some exotic place. I can remember one chilly winter's night, getting out of bed and with the aid of a chair, clambering on top of the white painted chest of drawers and pretending I was at the helm on the bridge of my ship, steering it through some fearful tempest. I stayed up there until I got really chilled (in fact not in imagination) then I handed over to the Bo'sun and climbed back down to my bunk in my cabin. Snuggled under my bedclothes again, I drank imaginary hot cocoa to warm me up.

So, come upstairs to the third floor where there was the night nursery, the day nursery, the spare room for visitors and a bathroom. The bathroom had a wonderful large bath, panelled in wood with a sort of hood at the wall end which was actually a shower with jets of water coming not only from the top but squirting out of the sides as well. I was never allowed to use the shower but Francis and Elizabeth did. Then there was a walk-in linen cupboard where Priscilla fell backwards off a stool when she was reaching up to a high shelf, shortly before we moved house. It was probably the start of her back problems later in life. I mustn't forget the coal bunker which was mainly empty of coal because the only coal fire was in the spare room and that was only lit when we had visitors which wasn't that often. The nursery had a gas fire.

Now up one more floor on uncarpeted stairs. Francis had his bedroom up there until Elizabeth went to boarding school. Next to his room was an empty room with a large table covered in boxes with tubes of paint and bottles of turpentine and other substances which my father used to clean and restore the pictures he bought at auctions and in antique shops. Frank spent many happy hours, humming away as he worked on his purchases and sometimes making exciting discoveries. I think he would much rather have earned his living as a picture restorer than as a chartered accountant.

The other two rooms on the top floor were empty except for some trunks in them. I loved playing up there and delving into the trunks which contained exotic clothing, parasols, pith helmets and various strange ornaments. I frequently dressed up in bits and pieces and I was permitted to play there provided I put everything back when I had finished. It was particularly light and airy at the top of the house as there was a glass cupola in the ceiling over the stairwell, through which the sun shone. I had no idea to whom the trunks belonged and no one enlightened me, probably some relatives who had come back from the East needing storage space. Nor do I know what happened to them when we left Royal Circus because they certainly did not come with us to Albert Terrace. Anyway by then I had lost interest in them.

As a small child, most of my day was confined to the top part of the house except when I was taken out for a walk in my pram in the afternoons. I had my meals in the nursery and I do remember my wooden high chair which could be put down low and the tray opened out into a big table top so I could sit and play with my toys. Bella ate with me and sometimes Bud would join us for tea if she got back from school in time. Francis or F.G. as he was sometimes called (Francis George) got home much later and probably had his own, much larger, tea by himself. I think that when he was 14 he started to have dinner at night with our parents. I loved my nursery which was a large, square room with dark blue cork flooring and a big walk-in cupboard where I kept my toys. Bella kept the tea there and also the cake tin. There was a big, round oak table and a small wardrobe with a long mirror on the door, in front of which I used to prance when wearing new clothes.

Adjoining the nursery was the night nursery where Bud and I used to sleep until she went away to school and then it became Francis's bedroom. I slept in the nursery in a bed that hooked up against the wall in the daytime, with curtains drawn over it. One of my earliest memories is gazing out of the nursery window in the evening, looking down on the street, waiting for the lamplighter to pass by and then stop and light the gas lamp which was practically opposite our house, with his long pole. Then I would breathe on the window and draw a picture of him with my finger. When the street lamps were electrified all the magic disappeared. I've always loved Stevenson's poem, *The Lamplighter*. I think our basement lighting was electrified around this time and the dark stone stair was finally illuminated by a bare bulb.

I think I was probably rather pampered when young and I was called Baby until I was seven, in fact until I went to school. Bella used to call me Doodles. Perhaps this is the place to tell you something about Bella – Bella Pennykid – who was with my parents for more than thirty years. She thought her family had immigrated from the Low Countries and certainly Pennykid was not a name I ever heard of or came across again. My father thought it might have been *Pfennigkind*. Her father was a miner and she was brought up outside Edinburgh and went to Dalkeith Academy where she did rather well, especially in maths. But the necessity of earning a living cut short her education. I think she was about seventeen when she first came to our house as a house tablemaid. I don't remember when she changed over to be my nanny. But the joke in our house was that when Francis was in need of help with his maths homework, it was Bella who helped him and not his accountant father!

There seemed to be this idea that I was a 'delicate child' but delicate in what way I am not sure – maybe it had something to do with my mother having Spanish flu when she was carrying me. I was definitely anaemic and to offset this I was fed raw steak, best steak scraped and made into delicate sandwiches between ice cream wafers. I loved them. In later years when asked what I would like for my special birthday lunch, I would invariably reply – "bloody steak". Maybe that is what set me off on a firmly carnivorous pattern of eating for the rest of my life.

I was brought up in a calm and harmonious atmosphere. Although the bulk of my care was undertaken by a nanny, my parents never seemed remote or uninvolved. I never heard them argue and although no doubt they had their problems like most married couples, they were not apparent. My father was a highly strung, intensely anxious man and inclined to presume disaster. On our summer holidays in the Highlands, if any of us were late home, we weren't just late, we had drowned in the loch or fallen over a precipice. I think it was quite hard for my mother who always maintained a great sense of calm about her but at the cost of internalising her own anxieties. Frank also had difficulties in expressing his feelings and I think he was able to relate to his children more easily when they were young. As an adolescent I didn't find him easy to approach with anything that was worrying me. It was not that he was unreceptive but because he got upset if things were not going too well for me. "Oh sweetheart," he would say, "I am sorry," and look as if he were about to burst into tears. My mum was much more matter of fact but not unsympathetic and I found that easier.

But I have the most wonderful early childhood memories of the bedtime stories my dad would tell me. He didn't read to me, he made them up. I would be in bed and after he had changed for dinner he would come upstairs to the night nursery and sit down on the chair beside my bed and say – "what is it to be tonight, Jacko or the Toy Shop?" Jacko was a mischievous monkey who created havoc in the jungle with his naughty tricks. He swung from tree to tree and threw down coconuts and got into scrapes generally with his fellow jungle dwellers. My father never repeated himself and I think he made the stories up as he went along. But the Toy Shop was my favourite. As soon as the proprietor locked up for the night all the toys became alive, the dolls, the teddies and other stuffed animals came down from the display shelves and had parties and dancing and the wooden buses and trains magically acquired engines. But they knew to the minute when they had to go back to their places and when the owner opened the door next morning everything was as he had left it. Sometimes my Mummy came up before the story was finished and she perched on Bud's bed (Bud came to bed much later of course) and when the story was finished my dad kissed me goodnight and went off downstairs. My mum waited until I had said my prayers (short and to the point) before she followed him. If the tablemaid hadn't rung the gong yet to signal that their dinner was in the dining room, they would stop off in the drawing room and one of them sat down at the piano and played, Frank usually Scottish airs by ear, Priscilla something more complicated from music. Many a night I'd drop off to sleep to the sound of piano music wafting up the stairs

Throughout my early childhood, Francis and Elizabeth (or Bud as she was often called because Francis when a little boy couldn't say Elizabeth and called her Lilybud) peopled my landscape intermittently. They were off to school first thing in the morning after breakfast, with our parents downstairs in the dining room, and didn't return until late afternoon or early evening. I led my self-contained nursery life upstairs, including all my meals. Who brought them up that long staircase from the kitchen, I can't remember, probably some long suffering tablemaid. But at the weekends I saw more of them and on wet Saturdays we had toffee-making sessions in the nursery. The gas fire which heated the room was in a fireplace enclosed by a high nursery fireguard. There was a tubular metal structure fixed to the back of the fire which came up to just above the fireguard and contained a gas ring for boiling kettles. On this we made toffee, at least Francis and Elizabeth did. I wasn't allowed to stir the mixture but my job was to hold the cup of cold water into which a speck of the mixture was spooned and there was the excitement of seeing whether it solidified in the water showing it was ready to be poured out into a shallow dish and left to cool.

When I was about five years old, we experienced a traumatic happening in the nursery. I was not very well for some reason and was being kept in bed. It was just before breakfast and I was sitting up in bed having my hair brushed by Bella. I think it must have been a cold winter's morning because not only was the gas fire on but there was also a small round one-bar electric fire plugged in behind Bella. Her nanny's uniform included a starched white apron and as she bent over to brush my hair, it stuck out behind her and one of the corners touched the electric stove and caught fire. She was suddenly aware of a ribbon of fire creeping up her back. In order not to frighten me, she laid down the hairbrush and went out of the room, closing the door behind her. From the landing she shouted down to my parents in considerable panic. My father was in his dressing room shaving and he came racing upstairs in his pyjamas. When he reached Bella she was apparently a pillar of flame. He shouted to my mother to bring blankets and proceeded to try and beat out the flames with his bare hands. My mother pulled the blankets off their big bed and when she got up to the landing they both enveloped Bella in the blankets and the flames were suffocated. Fortunately Bella was not too badly burnt, thanks largely to the thickness of her clothing and her corset. But my poor father was in screaming agony with his burned hands. Both our family doctor and Bella's panel doctor were phoned and came quickly to the house. I remember my father's hands being in bandages for weeks. When my mother came into the nursery to see what I was doing she apparently found me, white faced, sitting bolt upright in bed, my gaze transfixed on a smouldering scrap of cloth. She stamped it out (it left a burn mark on the cork floor) and unplugged the offending fire. I remember feeling a personal animosity against this inanimate object and I kicked it when I got out of bed because it had hurt my nanny and my daddy. A panel doctor, by the way, was the then equivalent of today's national health doctor.

There was another traumatic scene, enacted in the nursery some years later. I think I was about seven and may even have started school. I suffered quite a bit from sore throats, tonsillitis, etc. and it was decided that I should have my tonsils and adenoids removed and my parents thought it would be less disturbing for me if it happened at home. None of this was conveyed to me before the day of the operation when my mother came and told me just as I was waking up that I was going to have my tonsils removed that morning. Because of the operation I wasn't allowed any breakfast, but I was given a glass of warm milk. I lay petrified in bed listening to noises coming from the next-door nursery. These were sounds of the kitchen table being brought upstairs, to be covered by a large bath sheet and used as an operating table. My mother stayed with me and tried to read me a story but I wasn't listening. Then the front door bell rang and my mother left the room and very soon I heard men's voices coming up the stairs. My papa had left for the office and the other two were gone to school. I don't remember Bella around but I think all this may have happened after I had ceased to have a nanny and Bella had become our cook.

The next thing I knew our family doctor appeared in the room with my mother and sat down on my bed. Andrew Flett was our family doctor from since I could remember and remained my parents' doctor until after my father died in the 1950s. He was a tall, burly man and was not only our doctor but a family friend. He and the More boys had been great chums when they were growing up. He was a well known figure in Edinburgh and used to drive around in a brown Rolls coupé and he nearly always had the hood down whatever the weather. He was said to be very good to his panel patients and would often leave behind after a visit, a bottle of champagne or a grouse he had shot in the Highlands when on holiday. He told me that I was going to be put to sleep and that when I woke up I could have as much ice cream as I wanted. Then he picked me up in his arms and carried me into the nursery and laid me on this hard table.

There was a man I didn't know in a white coat (the surgeon) fiddling about with some things on a small table behind the 'operating table' and he didn't turn around when Dr Flett carried me in. Then suddenly a mask descended on my face and I was seized with panic. I reached up with both hands and tore it away. Taking advantage of the momentary confusion, I managed to slide off the table and run for the door. Dr Flett tried to grab me but I eluded him and ran to the other side of the round nursery table — escape being my sole object. I was soon back on the hard table but this time Dr Flett procured from my anxious Mama one of my father's large white handkerchiefs. This he dowsed with chloroform and held it gently over my nose and the next thing I knew I was back in my own bed with a bit of a sore throat and a taste of blood in my mouth. I enjoyed the fuss that was made of me afterwards and all the ice cream and cool drinks. Years later my mother told me she had had to give the two doctors stiff brandies before they left the house!

And so, Alex, these are just some aspects of my childhood. No doubt you find them a bit odd compared to your own well-organized and structured progression, but there are many paths to adulthood. I hope your Dad will bring you to see me again soon. In the meantime,

Lots of love
Granny Veronica

Dearest Damian

So you've succeeded in getting into art school in Brighton, I bet you're pleased. Congratulations! I've only been to Brighton twice. In fact I know the English south coast hardly at all, although your Mum did go to school in Worthing. My most vivid memory of that part of the world was being on an airfield near Folkestone during the Battle of Britain, in the summer of 1940.

Up until then my war had been relatively uneventful. Some months before war was declared I had signed up to be a driver in a women's ambulance corps. No demands were made on us except for an occasional meeting but we knew we were there to be called upon if, and when, war came. As far as the powers that be were concerned we were a pool of volunteers liable for duty whenever required. As a result, in August 1939, I was required to present myself at the Edinburgh Main Post Office to learn to be a teleprinter operator. I suppose the teleprinter was the forerunner of the fax. They were great unwieldy machines like giant typewriters. I was not a typist but could get by using two or three fingers. I can't remember a thing about my 'training' which took place, mornings only, for several days. When that was finished I was sent to Turnhouse RAF aerodrome on the outskirts of Edinburgh and which is now Edinburgh Airport. I didn't do a lot there, as far as I remember, except sit around or wash up dirty dishes from the airmen's mess. But it was where I heard the Prime Minister, Neville Chamberlain's broadcast, declaring war on Germany on September 3rd 1939. Germany had invaded Poland two days previously and had ignored France's and Britain's ultimatum to withdraw.

That was the end of peace as I knew it and the beginning of my six years war service. I was 20 years old. Next move was to a naval/air base on the north shore of the Firth of Forth. There were about ten of us altogether and we were billeted (compulsorily lodged) in private houses and boarding houses in the town of Rosyth. I shared an attic room with two others and as I didn't rush upstairs quickly enough I was unable to bag the single bed and had to share the double one with a much older woman who wore a pink satin nightdress and had her hair in a long, straggly, greyish pigtail. I would sleep clinging to my side of the bed – the mattress was lumpy and dipped in the middle. I've always hated pink satin ever since!

We started off on a six-hour night shift and this would entail being picked up around 2 a.m. by RAF transport and driven about three miles to the base where the teleprinter centre was. Mostly there were airmen at the other end of the teleprinters and once they had twigged that they were 'talking' to women, our teleprinters would print out cheeky messages. This somewhat livened up the dreary night watch and the sending out and receiving of messages about the movement of equipment and goods. I always remember one riveting invoice which read: *underpants, long, woollen, winter, airmen, for the use of.*

At some point, just before actual war was declared, I had been given a choice as to whether I wanted to go into the army or the air force. I thought the air force would be less stuffy, although I would really have liked to join the navy, but I wasn't given the option. At the start it all seemed very haphazard and unorganized. We had no proper uniforms and had been issued with navy blue pinnies which we wore over a shirt or pullover, an air force blue gabardine mac and a navy blue beret with a brass RAF badge on it – rather like the worst type of school uniform. I must say I was pretty cheesed off with the whole set-up and thought there must be some more interesting way I could contribute to the war effort than sit in front of a teleprinter which occasionally required my attention for the sending and receiving of boring invoices.

I had heard about the land girls and memories of long, wonderful, summer holidays on farms in the Highlands during my childhood, sparked off the thought that working on a farm could be infinitely preferable to what I was then doing. It would not have been too difficult to make the change as, at the start of the war, everything was fairly fluid and slapdash. At the same time there came a call for volunteer drivers to go to Finland to help the Finns who were about to be invaded by Russia. This I thought definitely sounded exciting and I made one or two tentative enquiries. In the event, I didn't follow up any of these openings because a signal arrived at our unit asking for drivers. I duly presented myself and after an initial driving test was accepted as an MT (motor transport) driver. But before being posted to a new unit, I had to undergo a short course of mechanics in an Edinburgh garage. I learned how to take an engine to pieces and put it together again and about various other aspects of the internal combustion engine. Luckily I never had to put any of this into practice and I now wouldn't know a big end from a brake shoe. While this was going on I was permitted to stay at home and I wallowed in hot baths, good food and my own bed (all to myself). At the end of the course I was given my posting and was sent to a Balloon Barrage Squadron in the village of Dalmeny, near South Queensferry on the Firth of Forth.

I was now firmly launched on my war service, no more second thoughts, unrealistic fantasies about Finland. I was an Aircraftwoman, second class, (ACW Plonk in service slang), the lowest form of life in the air force. We were quite a small unit whose operational job was to manage and maintain the huge silver sausages which floated in the sky attached to the ground by wires, protecting the shipping and the Forth Bridge from low level enemy attack. We women were, if I remember rightly, some ten WAAF (Women's Auxiliary Air Force) about five of whom were drivers and the rest worked in the Orderly

Room. We were billeted in cottages which ran down the side of the village green and my room mate was a girl called Eve. We clicked at once and became really good friends. She was a few years older than me and had an attractive and friendly demeanour and a great sense of humour. We cheered each other up during that long, perishingly cold first winter of the war.

The squadron had a fleet of six brand new Dodge vans (courtesy of our friends, not yet allies, the Americans). They were parked on the strip of village green along with some heavier duty vehicles and the green soon became a churned sea of mud and then like a skating rink when the hard packed snow froze over later in the winter. There was no petrol pump, so when we required petrol for our vehicles we went to the shed where the RAF petrol was stored in gallon tins. The storeman issued us with whatever we required against our signatures and the registration number of the van. I'll always remember the agony of unscrewing the stiff cap off the gallon tin on those icy mornings. Woollen gloves were useless and I soon acquired a leather pair. Then it dawned on me that I needed a funnel if I was not going to lose substantial trickles of petrol down my van and into the ground.

I was detailed to be the Stores Driver and my boss was a corporal to whom I had to report each morning. This meant driving out of the village and about two miles down the main Edinburgh road until I turned off left down a tree-lined avenue which led to the stable block of a large country house. The stable block had been commandeered by our squadron to house the stores and my corporal had made himself a very cosy billet in the erstwhile harness room. He was a neat, tidy little man with smooth, Brylcreamed fair hair. He often hadn't finished shaving when I reported for duty around 8.45. He was pleasant and friendly and it was he who introduced me to rum and Crabbies green ginger wine as a first-class tipple to keep the cold out. Later on in the winter when the snow lay thick on the ground, we would occasionally fortify ourselves with a nip of rum and ginger wine before setting forth on our morning errands and tasks! Although a regular airman my corporal did not seem too put out by having a woman driver and he refrained from the usual gender jokes which often pursued us girls and although not malicious and mainly good humoured, could be tedious. Depending on what was required on any particular day, I would either set out on my own or drive the corporal somewhere, especially if there should be a big load of stores to pick up from some airfield. I used to drive to Turnhouse and Grangemouth and sometimes across the Forth on the ferry to Rosyth. If I had finished the Store's business in the morning, after lunch, in the afternoon I joined the drivers 'pool' and we'd sit around the Orderly Room (which was housed in the school) until sent out on some task or other, generally very local.

By now we had been issued with proper uniforms and no longer felt like scarecrows, although we still didn't have great coats, only our gabardine macs. But our tunics and skirts, blue shirts and black ties, grey stockings and black walking shoes made us feel a whole lot smarter and more interested in our appearance. We were also able to change the RAF insignia on our berets for a WAAF one and later on we were given peaked caps as well. Apart from our outer garments we were issued with two sets of underwear which we did *not* wear except in the bitterest cold of that winter when we wore the issue bloomers or so-called 'passion killers' over our own pants for extra warmth.

Eve and I settled down to make the best of our billet. Our billetors (if that's the right word) were an oldish couple and the husband had been a miner in the local shale mines which were now defunct. It was a tiny one-storied cottage and we occupied the front room, two single beds, a table and two straight-backed chairs. There was a little iron fireplace in which, of an evening, our landlady would light a reluctant fire and encourage it with two damp logs which smoked and sizzled sadly all evening. We usually got in around 6 p.m. unless either of us was on a late run. (I didn't enjoy driving in the blackout with headlights the strength of weak torches.) We were brought our tea about six thirty, usually tinned salmon or tinned mackerel or baked beans, bread, marge and jam and a pot of tea. We ate this at our table and it was the only meal we had in our room. Breakfast we ate in the kitchen which was warmed by a coal fired range. The old man used to sit close to the range wearing his long johns and a shirt, coughing and sending forth streams of tobacco-coloured spittle accurately aimed at the spittoon a few inches from his feet while his missus, still in her nightdress, pared her corns and cut her toenails in close proximity to our breakfast table. Eve and I swallowed our bowls of porridge, followed by fried bread and tomatoes with occasionally a limp rasher of bacon, as fast as we could, stuffed in a slice of bread and jam and washed it all down with a mug of scalding tea.

Conversation was minimal, we needed to fortify ourselves to face the wintry conditions outside where we tanked up our vehicles with petrol at the start of the day. The lavatory was out in the yard, mercifully it was a flush one but we were provided with a chamber pot in case we were taken short in the night. In the mornings we washed in the scullery at the sink, usually stuffed with the previous evening's supper dishes, floating herring or kipper bones etc. As you can imagine it was a quick flannel over our faces and a hasty brushing of our teeth. Some evenings a week we took an enamel basin with warm water into our room and did some more serious washing.

Breakfast and tea were usually the only meals Eve and I ate together. Mid-day dinner was ready around 12.30 but if either of us were not back our helpings would be put on a plate and shoved into the oven to keep warm, flattened-down spuds and swedes and a piece of unidentifiable meat or fish, or, now and again, a greyish stew with dumplings. I was usually so ravenously hungry I was ready to wolf down anything, including the suet pudding which followed. True, we sometimes had tinned fruit and custard and very occasionally Mrs Watts would make a rice pudding which was really good.

As I said before the great plus of these months at Dalmeny was my friendship with Eve. In the evenings, over our tinned salmon or whatever it was, we mulled over the day's happenings and the latest squadron gossip and we got to know a bit about each other's lives to date. The first thing we did when we had finished eating was to clean our shoes and buttons and only very rarely did we omit this chore. On the whole our landlady looked after us reasonably well, according to her lights. At least she was friendly and didn't seem to resent us. I don't know what they got paid but I suppose it made a slight increase in their small income.

I remember that in January 1940 I developed a very septic throat and ran a high temperature. The M.O. banished me back to bed with pills and ordered me to drink a lot. Mrs Watts procured a bottle of Glucozade for me and she kept popping her head round the door, saying "are ye better the noo, dearie?" Then my mother came to collect me in the car (it had yet to be laid up) after I had been granted a week's sick leave, the M.O. thinking I would get better more quickly at home. Mrs Watts said to my mama, "she could'nae hae been better looked after in her ain hame." I do not remember Priscilla's reply who was viewing for the first time where I was actually living. This was the other big plus of that winter in Dalmeny – I was near home. For my 48 hours monthly pass I went to Edinburgh on the bus from South Queensferry and spent two blissful days, wearing civilian clothes, enjoying hot baths and eating good, recognizable food cooked by dear Bella and regaling my parents with stories about life in the Air Force.

I don't think either Elizabeth or Francis were home at this time. Elizabeth was still in Dunkeld with the Atholls where she remained until the Duke's death. Francis had been to his OCTU (Officer Cadet Training Unit) and while there had been diagnosed as having a tubercular lung and had been sent to the Tor-na-dee Sanatorium near Aberdeen. The only time that he wore his officer's uniform was on the train journey north. A distressing experience for a young man, most of whose friends were all joining up.

How quickly my hours of freedom sped by and I was back on the late evening bus, crowded with sailors, some of them very drunk indeed, bound for South Queensferry. Now and again on the few occasions I had a run which brought me into Edinburgh, I would sneak out to Albert Terrace for a cup of tea or a bite of lunch and thus add some illicit mileage to my day's log. I disliked my Dodge van, it didn't seem to me to be particularly driver friendly and when the snow fell it had no hold on the road and when the snow froze it was positively lethal. I used to crawl along down the icy main road with my heart hammering in my rib cage. Luckily there was practically no traffic but I felt a great sense of relief when I turned off down the drive towards the Stores where my corporal would revive me with a little nip of rum. I cannot now quite remember how long the snow and ice lasted but it was certainly weeks rather than days. On a couple of the coldest nights when our room felt arctic, Eve and I went to bed without taking our clothes off. We removed our skirts and tunics and put on an extra pullover and I remember putting the bedside mat on my bed for extra warmth.

It was a strange winter that first winter of the war. Germany had over-run Poland and then there was a lull. Nothing much happened, it was known as the 'phony war'. We became lax about carrying our gasmasks and still more our tin hats – people said it would be over by Christmas but of course it wasn't. In the quiet of the night I used to wonder what Albert and my subsequent boyfriend, Arthur, might be doing. It was difficult for me to think of them as the enemy, especially as I might, just might, have married Arthur. And I would think about the Varnbüler family in Stuttgart. Like everyone else I also hoped the war would soon be over, but one cannot live in dreams and I was fully occupied with the conditions of my day to day life.

Finally the winter receded and spring arrived. The Germans invaded the Low Countries and I was posted to Grangemouth, some miles to the north. It was a proper peacetime RAF station and they required another driver. Why me? I'd no idea. Anyway I had my marching orders and 24 hours in which to pack my kit and say goodbye to my mates. I was particularly sorry to say goodbye to Eve. We were to meet occasionally throughout the war (she became a Code and Cyphers officer) and she came to the luncheon party Tom and I gave after we were married. But eventually we lost touch, she was a bad correspondent and I wasn't much better.

I don't remember a lot about my time at Grangemouth. It was my first experience of a proper aerodrome and being part of an established MT section. I was the only female but I don't remember being given a hard time. I didn't live on the aerodrome but was billeted out again, about ten minutes walk away. I was the only billetee. I remember nothing about this billet apart from numerous caged canaries to whom my landlords were always chirping away. I think it may have been of a rather higher standard than Dalmeny. I had a little Hillman truck to drive with a tarpaulin over the back like a hood which flapped about as I drove. There was no messing about with petrol tins, we had a proper pump.

One thing I do remember was one day having to pick up the duty officer to take him to the airmen's mess to inspect the dinner and listen to any complaints. He was late and didn't turn up at the pick-up point. My sergeant told me to go to the officers' mess and drag him out. I went to the mess and asked if the D.O. was there. A young Flying Officer detached himself from the group around the bar and followed me out. When he got into the vehicle beside me he said – "you should always salute when you come into an officers' mess." What, salute a crowd of young men drinking round a bar? Well, mate, I thought, you shouldn't be late on duty. There were two ways to get to the airmens' mess, a rough potholed track across a field and a reasonable macadam road which was a longer way round. I chose the dirt track and drove as fast as I could without overturning my shaky little vehicle. When we arrived the duty officer said, "weren't you driving rather fast?" I replied, "I thought you wouldn't want to waste time... sir.' I drove him back to his mess at a very sedate pace along the tarmac road.

I suppose it was the first time I had come across RAF 'bull'. On our balloon squadron we had been very relaxed. Nearly all the officers were from the Reserve and had just left civvy street, many of the men were also volunteers. Only the N.C.O.s were regulars and I think they regarded both the reserve officers and the women in the same light, not fully efficient and needing an eye kept on them. But it was a friendly almost paternal eye. The other thing I remember about Grangemouth was washing officers' cars in my free time, 2/6 a car (about 15p) which helped to augment my meagre pay.

I had by now been promoted to an Aircraftwoman, first class, but it did not affect my pay, about 10/- (50p) a week. I always used to think pay parades were an excessive amount of spit and polish to collect a very small amount of money.

Being at Grangemouth still enabled me to go home for my 48-hour passes, although it was quite a bit further away from Edinburgh. Occasionally I might have an official run into the city and if I happened to be alone I'd pay a quick visit to my parents. No mobile phones in those days and so of course sometimes my parents weren't always at home. But Bella would make me a cup of something and I'd chat to her for half an hour and say hello to my little Cairn terrier, Freuchie.

I seem to have made rather a digression in order to return to telling you how I landed up on the English south coast in the summer of 1940. But that's what the foregoing all leads up to. One day a signal arrived in the Orderly Room at Grangemouth asking for the names of any personnel who had a knowledge of German. I gave my name to the Flight Sergeant who said, "how come you know German?" and my fellow drivers thought it very odd. I didn't think any more about it and then after about a week I was sent for by the Orderly Room. A puzzled looking Flight Sergeant told me I had to go to London for an interview, he didn't know what for but he gave me the address where I had to report in two days' time. So I set off with a return travel warrant in my pocket on the night train from Edinburgh to London, sitting up four a side, dozing off uncomfortably and wishing that my smoking co-travellers (mainly soldiers) would have the decency to go out and smoke in the corridor. I arrived bleary eyed at Euston and took myself off to the station hotel for some breakfast and a bit of a spruce up before presenting myself for this mystery interview. I had been given some maintenance money from the Orderly Room petty cash fund but also, on my fleeting visit home on my way to the train, my dad had slipped me a couple of pounds thus allowing me to order a much more ample breakfast than my RAF subvention would have allowed. Afterwards I decided to take a taxi and arrived outside an imposing looking building in a street off Whitehall at 9.45.

It was obviously an Air Ministry building as it was humming with blue uniforms. But it was a rather elderly civilian porter who received me. "You'll be one of those for upstairs," he said and ushered me into a creaky lift. When we got to whatever floor it was, he took me down a long corridor and showed me into a room where there were already four other WAAF seated on chairs round the wall. Eventually we became eight, all other ranks except for one corporal. We none of us knew one another and to begin with everyone eyed everyone else with suspicion. Then someone said – "Does anyone know what this is all about?" That broke the ice and we all started chatting to whoever we were sitting next.

There was another room beyond us and at 10 a.m. sharp the door opened and a WAAF sergeant came into our waiting room. She was pleasant and friendly and explained that we would be called individually in alphabetical order, that first our German would be tested and then we would be told about the job. "And don't forget to salute," she said before she disappeared, closing the door behind her. A few minutes later it was opened again and the first candidate was summonsed. We followed her with sympathetic eyes as she disappeared through the door. Finally my turn came.

I went into a smallish room where five people were sitting behind a large table, three male officers, the WAAF sergeant and a civilian. One of the officers had what we used to call scrambled eggs on his cap brim, in other words, gold braid, which meant he was very senior. I threw up my best salute and the Group Captain (or whatever he was) said "sit down" indicating the hard-back chair placed just off centre in front of the table. I took a seat but wasn't quite sure whether I should be sitting to attention or sitting more relaxed so I attempted something mid way between. I crossed my legs and then hastily uncrossed them again.

The WAAF sergeant was the first to address me – in German. Where was I from? What was my job in my unit? Where had I learned German? What sort of journey had I had to London? Rather aimless chatter (I thought) as I answered her questions in what I hoped was faultless German but probably wasn't. She was very relaxed and friendly and was obviously trying to put me at ease. Then there was a pause and the sergeant glanced down the table towards the civilian and gave a brief nod. I shifted in my chair and waited. The next to speak was the civilian. He was hesitant in manner and kept on taking off and putting back on the cap of his fountain pen as he spoke. If this was a job description it was delivered in the most obfuscatory manner and left me little the wiser. He mumbled on about important secret work, vital to the war effort but he didn't actually say what it was. All those engaged on it would have to sign the Official Secrets Act. "Do you have any questions?" "Could you say a little bit more about what we actually have to do?" I asked innocently. "That will have to wait until and if you are selected," came the reply. So what more could I say? Then one of the RAF officers piped up. "It is voluntary and if you are selected you will be made a sergeant, so in order not to waste everyone's time we would like to know

now if you would volunteer." So what could I reply to that but "Yes, sir, I would." The other officer dismissed me. "Return to your unit, Aircraftwoman More, and you will hear in due course." I got up from my chair, saluted smartly and exited.

In the waiting room there were three more to go. The rest were chatting away quietly, comparing notes and trying to fathom what on earth it was we'd be called upon to do. "Maybe we're going to be beautiful spies," said a rather glamorous looking blonde whose hair was longer than regulation length. "Fat chance," snapped a sturdy Newcastle lass. "More likely to be something dead boring." We had come to no conclusion by the time the last one had been interviewed. The sergeant came back into the waiting room and started to shoo us all off, making sure everyone had a travel warrant to get them back to their unit. And so we drifted out of the building into the pale sunshine of London in spring. When we reached Whitehall we went our separate ways, one of the girls was also going to Euston so we went together on the underground.

When I got back to Grangemouth my mates in the transport section were all agog to know what my interview had been about. There wasn't much I could tell them and I more or less put the whole thing out of my mind and life carried on as usual. Then about two weeks later I was told to report to the Orderly Room. The Flight Sergeant was on his feet behind his desk, frowning down on a sheet of paper that lay there. He looked up and saw me, picked up the sheet of paper and waved it towards me, glowering. "A signal's just come from Air Ministry, it says you've been posted to RAF Hawkinge, near Folkstone and…" (here he almost choked) "…you've been promoted to sergeant. If you're a sergeant then I'm a Group Captain."

Poor man, his sense of injury was understandable. He was a regular airman and had probably been promoted stage by stage until he worked his way up to the rank of Flight Sergeant and here was this whipper snapper of a girl apparently being handed the rank of sergeant on a plate. Still, that was his problem – I was all excited at the prospect of change. He recovered himself sufficiently to organise what was necessary. I was given a travel warrant to Folkestone and told to contact the R.T.O. (Railway Travel Officer) when I arrived so he could arrange for onward transport to Hawkinge. I received a chit for the stores so that I could be issued with my sergeant's stripes which I was instructed to be wearing when I arrived in Folkestone. I was also given a 24-hour leave pass which meant I could go home for the night to say goodbye to my parents before travelling south by day the following morning. When I got home I sewed on my stripes but had to unpick them because they were squint and my mother sewed them on correctly.

So there I was, Damian, poised to go to the south coast of England. RAF Hawkinge was a small fighter aerodrome on the edge of the Downs above Folkestone, looking out over the English Channel. On a clear day one could just discern on the horizon the shadowy outline of Cap Gris Nez which since the fall of France had now become enemy territory. So it was with the feeling of being in the front line that we all (about 20 WAAF sergeants) retired to bed that first night in the unoccupied Officers' Married Quarters where we were housed. At first light, around 5 a.m. the next morning, we were awakened by the sound of the Spitfire squadron arriving from an inland base to await the day's action. At breakfast the air raid warning sounded and we grabbed our toast and tin hats and belted for the air raid shelters, or trenches as they were called, while the squadron roared into action above. Happily we were not this time the target and very soon the all-clear sounded.

We still did not know what we were doing there until mid-morning when we had to parade and were marched in a squad past the hangars and other station buildings, down a leafy lane just off the perimeter to a small country house called Maypole Cottage. Once there all was revealed to us. The house was covered in a network of aerials and inside, the rooms were full of radio receiving sets. At each receiver sat Air Force

66

personnel, both male and female, wearing headphones and twiddling nobs and every now and again writing in big log books. This was the secret work we had been selected for, radio operators to listen in to the Luftwaffe's open speech radio communication between aircraft and aircraft, and aircraft and their base. Big Hallicrafter receiving sets, supplied like the Dodge vans by our American friends, still not yet our allies, dominated the room space. There was a lot of fine tuning required on VHF so one needed to have light, sensitive fingers and also an ability to direct one's hearing to the German voices through all the atmospherics and extraneous radio interference. I became quite adept at scribbling down the dialogue of German pilots engaged in full battle with our Spitfires overhead. We wrote on alternate lines in our log book and when there was a lull in the action or just before we went off watch, we wrote the translation underneath, of what we had transcribed.

All our log sheets were sent off daily to somewhere in the Air Ministry to be interpreted and assessed. From the repeated code words and other non-variables and in conjunction with Morse code log sheets, a picture began to be built up of the formation and bases of the German Air Force. After noting an aircraft's call sign we wrote down everything we could hear – comments, information, warnings, swearing, shouts of triumph when one of ours was shot down and finally their last screams of terror and anguish (and occasionally their prayers) when they were hit and started to spiral earthwards. Most died with their mother's, wife's or sweetheart's name on their lips. Very few crashed to their death exclaiming a defiant *Heil Hitler*.

One fine August afternoon on my off-duty time, I was lying on the grass in the garden enjoying the sunshine and snatching some momentary peace. Looking up into the clear, blue sky, I spied an aircraft way high up. Quite suddenly it started to sign write in the sky and transcribed an enormous swastika right over our aerodrome before it sped off. I sat up and saw some airmen over by one of the hangars, also looking skywards. I got up and went over to them. "What's that all about?" I asked. "Search me," one of them replied, he shrugged and they all went back to their tasks.

We were being bombed on a daily, sometimes twice daily basis but on the following day August 12th we suffered the father and mother of an attack. It was in the morning, just after breakfast and when we at last emerged from the trenches we saw that the damage was extensive. Several hangars were stoved in, aircraft destroyed and the airfield pitted with bomb craters. There had been low flying Stukas in the attack, raking the ground with machine gun fire just for good measure and we had heard them from the trenches. Apart from the London Blitz this was as near to the shooting war as I was to get. Somehow the Blitz seemed more impersonal, I didn't feel I was being personally attacked whereas at Hawkinge I did. And of course we all were – the whole objective being to put our aerodrome out of action. We were lucky that only one person was killed, a member of the ground staff. In addition, of course, I was in daily contact with these pilots who were attacking us. I knew their voices, their manner of speech and humour (if any) and I had formed my personal opinions, some pilots I liked and some I disliked.

I will also never forget going on watch when a raid had just started up. How insubstantial my tin hat felt as the shrapnel tinkled down around us marching along that leafy lane to Maypole Cottage. If a raid had already started before we left then we went down into the trenches and those on duty in Maypole Cottage would have to hang on and continue working until the relief watch turned up. On the whole everyone stood up to these attacks extraordinarily well. We had three girls who became hysterical and the M.O. recommended that they should be moved elsewhere. Mostly we women were no less stoical than the men, sometimes more so. There was one officer, I forget from which section, who rolled himself into the foetal position and remained inert and speechless until the all-clear sounded. Some of the airmen played cards, many of the WAAF busied themselves with small, domestic tasks, darning stockings, sewing on the missing button, filing our nails. It may have seemed absurd, even pointless, but these mundane domestic chores helped to quieten our nerves.

It was at Hawkinge that I met Rosemary, Horstmann as she was then and Waters which she later became. We shared so many war experiences and were together for over two years. It was a friendship which endured for the rest of our lives, until 2004 when sadly Rosemary died. We were on the same watch and so spent our off-duty time together. Mostly we took the bus into Folkestone because by being off the aerodrome during the day, we escaped the raids. We enjoyed ourselves wandering round the town, doing a bit of shopping, having a sandwich and a beer, or an ice cream – we felt quite rich on our sergeant's pay – and eyeing up the male Service personnel who like us were off duty and strolling around. Then one evening when we returned to base, the chap on sentry duty said to us, "Your lot have gone." "What do you mean – gone?" "Gone, taken off in a lorry – lock, stock and barrel."

There had been some talk of withdrawing our listening post further inland, but nothing had been decided. From the guard house we went to the orderly room to find out what was afoot. We were informed that all the WAAF sergeants had been removed to an unknown destination and that we were to follow the next morning. They knew we were in Folkestone and had alerted the Folkestone police to find us. This they had failed to do although we must have been pretty obvious in the streets as there weren't that many WAAF around. We went to our quarters and found that our mates had very kindly packed all our belongings and taken off our kit bags. They left nothing, not even a toothbrush! As fate would have it there was a raid that night and Rosemary and I had to go down to the trenches wrapped in blankets to cover our nakedness. The next morning we were taken to Folkstone railway station and we got a train to Sevenoaks from where we rang a number we had been given and RAF transport came to pick us up. We rejoined the others in the village of West Kingsdown, tucked away high up on the Kentish Downs. All the radio equipments had been transferred and set up in a small villa and a disused toy factory, it was already operational. We were delighted to be reunited with our kit bags and we were put in a comfortable billet with friendly people and that night we went on duty.

And so my stint on the south coast came to an end. Life became more peaceful and our ragged nerves had a chance to recover. It was not because we were women in the battle zone that we had been withdrawn inland but because the organisation of our work was being seriously hampered by continual raids. The reception was excellent where we were now stationed and our field of listening extended. The only visible sign of war we experienced now was the occasional dog fight overhead between a Spitfire and a Messerschmitt and later on, the drone of enemy bombers on daylight raids (later abandoned) flying towards London and other cities.

As I write this letter to you it has suddenly become very apparent to me how highly significant were those nine months I spent in Germany. If I hadn't known German I would never have got the job I was doing and if I hadn't been doing that job I would probably never have gone to Cairo and would not have met your grandfather and none of you would have been here. Serendipity plays a considerable part in our lives, does it not?

Anyway. I'd better sign off now from this lengthy epistle. Enjoy your course, Damian, and have a fruitful time in Brighton.

> Lots of love
> > from
> > > your reminiscing g'ma
> > > Veronica

Dearest Steph

Here I am back home again. I really did enjoy my visit to you in Brindisi and thank you for looking after me so well and showing me so much. The highlight of course was our excursion to Conversano. How strange it was to return after more than fifty years to that little hill town in southern Italy where I spent the last six months of my overseas war service. When you and I arrived there, I didn't recognise the place at first. The modern town built on the flat around the base of what was once a small hill village, was so much larger than I remembered it, that I was confused. But when we walked up the steps from where you had parked the car and came out on to the wide space in front of the cathedral, memories came flooding back. The smell of the wood smoke which lingered in the narrow streets, women in black shawls, ragged children and the mysterious looking small groups of men in long cloaks and black hats who gathered at street corners and who at any moment one expected to break into a Verdi chorus. That is all gone now, everything looking so prosperous, sanitised and gentrified.

I came to Conversano after two years service in Cairo, in Heliopolis to be precise. After two years working in the Air Ministry in London I volunteered for overseas service and was posted to Egypt in January 1942. By then I had been commissioned and was now a Section Officer. I was working in Wireless Intelligence but no longer glued to a wireless set. Instead, I investigated decoded log sheets and mined what information I could from them about the bases, movements, and possible intentions of the German Luftwaffe. My friend Rosemary followed me to London from the Kentish Downs and we were both engaged on the same work. We shared a flat in St. George's Drive at the back of Victoria Station. It had all its windows blown out one noisy night and the glass was replaced with tin which made the whole place dark and miserable. Added to which the tin rattled when there was a wind. We had been considering moving out of central London because although travelling would add to our working day, at least we would get more peaceful nights. The suburbs might get the odd bomb dropped on them but they were not targets like central London. The arrival of the tin finally activated us and we found a lovely flat in West Hill, Putney. It was in a large, detached Victorian house standing in a beautiful big garden with big, old elm trees.

However we were not to leave Victoria without one final drama. We were between flats and living temporarily in a boarding house in Eccleston Square where I subsequently bought a flat in the sixties. It was a particularly noisy night and the Pimlico Guild Hall, which was next door, received a direct hit from a huge bomb, known as a landmine. The blast brought our roof down on top of us and blew out the stairs for five houses along. We were 'sleeping' as usual in our beds. Early on in the Blitz I had decided that if I was going to be killed I would rather die in my bed and gave up going down to the basement. We were on the fifth floor, the top floor. We had to climb over piles of rubble to get to the window (a glassless gash in the wall) to shout down to the wardens below that we were stranded. Rosemary thought that she ought to change into her silk pyjamas to be rescued and I remembered I had painted my toenails an exotic pale blue. What neither of us realised was that we were coal-black from head to foot with all the dirt that had spewed out of the destroyed roof and nobody could have cared less what we looked like nor what colour our toenails were. Nor did we know at the time that it wasn't only our house that was without stairs, and how slender our chances of rescue were.

I had never been so scared in my life, the raid continued and every time a bomb fell the shell of the building shook as if it might collapse. They had bombed us, why couldn't they go home now? But we were lucky. After about an hour, help arrived in the shape of three brave, stalwart auxiliary firemen. They had walked along the coping stone until they located us and then let down a rope and hauled us up through the broken roof on to the coping stone beside them. Telling us to look towards the roof and not the street below, they led us, holding on to their broad belts, along this narrow ledge, until we reached a house where there were stairs. Years later, in peacetime London, I would look up at these ledges and wonder how on earth we had done it.

When we reached a house with stairs, we had to be carried down as they were covered in broken glass and we were barefooted. Fireman's lift is not the most comfortable way to be carried, like a sack of potatoes over the shoulder! Once down on the pavement, lit up from fires in the gardens, our rescuers wanted to know who we were and whether we had any friends or relatives nearby. We explained our identity although we had nothing to show for it and I said I had an aunt in Wimbledon. It was around 3 a.m. and our firemen were a bit nonplussed as to what to do with us. Waves of bombers were still dropping their loads but they said the air raid shelter below the local bus station was overflowing. Then one of them said, "I know it's not allowed but I think we should take you to our sub-station in Belgravia and the girls can look after you." And that's how I got to ride on a fire engine for the first and last time in my life. Admittedly it was a very small fire engine but it was exciting racing through the streets and as we crossed Buckingham Palace Road I asked if I could ring the fire bell and as we sped on I pulled on the rope which made the bell ring.

We were left in a mews off Belgrave Square and it was like arriving in heaven. The girls couldn't have done more for us. We were plied with sweet tea, well laced with whisky and then they filled a metal bath with steaming water and we were able to wash off at least the top layer of dirt and become a pale shade of grey. They lent us pyjamas and binned our filthy rags, then tucked us up in camp beds in a room below the office where the night's noises sounded more distant. We dozed fitfully until morning. Then I rang Aunt Sophie in Wimbledon and told her of our plight. Very soon we were in a taxi in our borrowed night-clothes plus cardigans and two or three pounds which the girls had lent us. The taxi driver appeared as if he was quite used to passengers with dirty faces in their pyjamas and we told him about our night's adventure on the drive out to Wimbledon. When he dropped us off in Lingfield Road, he refused to accept his fare.

We spent three days with Sophie, endlessly scrubbing ourselves while she fed us, gave us strong drink and, most importantly, sent us to bed on the first night dosed with very strong sleeping pills. We slept for 18 hours and that sleep, I am sure saved us from delayed shock and trauma. Two of our brave firemen were members of the B.B.C. Symphony Orchestra, one was a flautist and I think the other played the cello. Once Rosemary and I were established in our new flat in Putney, we invited them and their wives round for a celebration. They were subsequently awarded the George Medal for rescuing us.

But to come back to Conversano. By the summer of 1943 the war had progressed into Europe and it became abundantly clear that our listening posts in Egypt were now too far behind the front line to be operationally useful. And so talk of moving 276 Wing to Europe became the talk of the day. The C.O. went off with other senior officers to inspect possible sites. Greece seemed to be a firm favourite and many of us were on the point of taking up Greek lessons when the name of Conversano cropped up – a hill town in Apulia. And Conversano it was – all highly secret of course.

So, our lives in Egypt were coming to an end. Tom and I had been so lucky being together for so long. The Wing was to be divided into advance and rear parties. As luck would have it, Tom was with the advance party and I was in the rear.

Rosemary, having just parted from her companion of many months who was in the Army and had been posted back to the UK, was also in the rear party.

At the time quite a number of familiar faces went missing, posted back to the Air Ministry or Bletchley Park. At 6 a.m. one autumn morning, I kissed Tom goodbye in our flat and then heard the lorry pull away from the house and fade away into the distance.

Having lived for so long in Heliopolis we had gathered a good deal of moss in the shape of possessions. Tom had packed everything he could not take to Italy in a big trunk which I had the task of sending off to the UK. My own surplus to requirements belongings, I put into two large cardboard boxes and sent them off to Edinburgh where they arrived after many months. I gave notice at the flat and became a paying guest with a Syrian family at the other end of the street. They had a roomy first floor flat overlooking the racecourse.

Tom and I were able to keep in contact by using the official post bag to which our superiors kindly turned a blind eye. Now and again we sent letters 'by hand' if there was someone in transit in either direction. There was very little work to do and I mostly did my Italian homework while on duty. I had embarked on an Italian course at a language school in Heliopolis and I felt I was making some progress. Italian fired me with greater enthusiasm than Arabic of which I had learned barely 150 words.

Eventually we were given a firm date of departure after a series of false alarms. Before leaving I took a few days leave because I thought it was a shame to leave Egypt without having visited Luxor. It had been out of bounds for several months because of malaria, but the ban had been lifted and I went there for a long weekend, travelling down there on the Friday night train and coming back on the Monday one. It seemed so strange to be travelling without Tom but I was glad I had made the effort to see these magnificent ruins so full of the mystery and symbolism of the Pharonic civilisation.

We were to be ready by 7.30 a.m. Rosemary, having given up her flat, was without a bed for the last night. She came and shared mine. The transport took us to Cairo railway station where we joined the rest of the party on the platform, four officers and couple of NCOs and about 50 chaps. We were a neat compact little group and everyone was in a good humour. Rosemary and I had the straps around our holdalls notched up a hole or two by male muscle. When we arrived in Alexandria, the men went off to a transit camp and Rosemary and I were parked in a boarding house on the sea front. We were given a telephone number which we had to ring every day at nine in the morning to find out whether we had a free day. And so we settled down to wait for the boat. It was cold and wet and the Mediterranean looked unfriendly. We read, wrote letters, went to the cinema, visited museums and the very sparse archaeological diggings that were going on at the time. When very fed up, we went to a cafe and had hot chocolate and cream cakes.

Then one day we rang and were told – tomorrow. What excitement! I was longing to see Tom and all this hanging about had been most frustrating. But now we were on our way at last. The boat was very different from the troopship I had travelled out on to Freetown. It was much smaller and more importantly it was DRY, i.e. no alcohol. At the start of the war there had been some calamitous happenings at sea which might have been less fatal if those in charge had not been the worse for drink, and troopships were very soon made 'dry'. But this boat had also been a cruise liner and it was still staffed by Javanese stewards.

We were a bag of mixed nationalities – Americans, Free French, some Poles and a contingent of ATS from Palestine. The first day at sea was calm and I was happy to be on a boat and going somewhere I wanted to be. On the second day one of those typical Mediterranean squalls blew up suddenly and the boat pitched about mercilessly. Rosemary took to her bunk and the noises coming from the ATS's cabins were not encouraging. We were not allowed to close our cabin doors, we could put them on the latch but they were not to be shut. I've forgotten what the reason was, something to do with the possibility of being torpedoed, I think, but certainly it let in all the surrounding noises of people throwing up. Mercifully the German Navy was now no longer dominant in the Mediterranean (or anywhere) but, on the evening of the third day, we were ordered to the boat stations wearing our life belts. The cause was an unidentified aircraft, and there we sat for two hours until we were released without incident. I felt I could have done with something stronger than a glass of lemonade to pull myself together again.

On the afternoon of the fourth day we sailed into Taranto harbour. As we approached the dock I leaned over the rail in a fever of anticipation. We had quite a party from 276 Wing to welcome us, headed by the Wing Commander. As we edged in I scanned the landing stage hopefully. Yes, there he was, sitting on a bollard. Trust Tom to have got himself on the welcoming party! Once we were safely ashore with our luggage, we piled into the waiting lorries and drove out of Taranto as dusk was falling. We drove along twisting narrow roads with dry stone walls on either side. Through the gaps in the flapping tarpaulin which covered the backs of the lorries, we could just make out in the gloom, the gnarled trunks of olive trees. It felt so different – the scents, the sounds and the air around us. We had left the East behind and were now in Europe – it was a good feeling.

And so, Stephanie, that is how I arrived in Conversano towards the end of January 1944. I was there until June when Rosemary, Tom and I, among others, all went back to the UK on the same troopship from Naples. It was a wonderful six months. The mud and the snow receded and spring came, bringing with it the burgeoning blossom of the almond trees and carpets of variegated wild flowers. Often on a Saturday at lunchtime a group of us would take off on bicycles with a picnic, and cheap litre bottles of red wine in our haversacks.

The picnic you and I had in that field after we left Conversano reminded me of all those other picnics so many years ago. Sometimes Tom and I hired a pony and trap when we wanted to go out on our own and we explored a lot of the surrounding country in this way.

The worst of the war had by-passed Conversano but although they were not shell-shattered nor starving, the people had very little. The only thing I remember buying in a shop were buttons. They had the most wonderful selection, all colours, all sizes, and some of them even looked hand painted. I wouldn't be at all surprised if I didn't still have a Conversano button tucked away somewhere. Then there were the *cantine*, behind a dingy curtain and down rough steps to a small cellar where we drank rough red wine for the equivalent of sixpence a litre. There was a shortage of glasses so we were given a bottle of wine and one glass on the table and we took it in turns drinking.

It was great that through your initiative I managed to make contact with a fairly distant member of the family of the wine grower with whom Tom had been officially billeted (and myself not so officially). The WAAF were housed in an empty, rather cheerless villa down below near the mess and I stayed there as little as possible, usually only when I was WAAF duty officer. By talking to this chap I made contact with when I was with you, I got information (as you know) about what had happened to some of the people we used to know. The wine grower who had been a widower was now dead and his son who was five years old when we knew him had become a globe trotter. The resplendent maid, Angelina who we thought also comforted the widower, had emigrated to the Argentine. The only person we had kept in touch with was the Mother Superior who gave Tom and me Italian lessons and who came and stayed with us at Monk's Hatch after the war. She was a lively, highly intelligent lady and was promoted in the Church hierarchy to some important post in Rome.

I hope to see you in Mallorca later on in the summer, Steph. In the meantime enjoy the rest of your teaching stint in Brindisi. Thank you again for having me to stay and enabling me to re-visit the shadows of my past.

Much love,
your loving grandma
Veronica

Dearest David

1 was so pleased to hear from your Mum and Dad about the safe arrival of Sophie Elizabeth, my love and congratulations to you and Helen. My first great-granddaughter!

It has just occurred to me that I too had a miscarriage like Helen before I had my first child. It happened at the start of the journey we made through Europe in 1946. After we were married in January of that year we moved from our nice flat in Putney, which we couldn't really afford, to a rather grotty room plus kitchen in a boarding house in Handel Street, which was on the fringes of Bloomsbury. We had been planning for some time to go on a trip to some of the countries in post-war Europe, for Tom to take photographs and me to write articles about them. We were not thinking of starting a family at that time so I never thought when I didn't feel too well that maybe I was pregnant. It wasn't anything very specific, I just felt 'off'. However we made our preparations for departure and wound up our affairs in London.

Owing to his war wounds Tom had been given a grant of £200 to help him set up as a freelance photographer. With this money he had bought a second-hand little Morris 5 cwt. van and in this vehicle we intended to travel Europe. Into the back of the van we packed the photographic equipment, rudimentary camping gear such as a spirit stove, our two wartime camp beds and a tarpaulin to shelter us from the weather. About the beginning of July we drove down to Dover and got on the boat for Ostende, starting off on our adventure full of anticipation.

We first went to Antwerp to stay with a Flemish couple who had befriended Tom during his wartime stay in Antwerp. The husband was an artist, and his wife, Nadine, was a very pretty woman with a sweet nature, they had a little boy of about five.

I didn't feel too great, very tired and a bit sick. Nadine, who was very concerned and kind to me, asked me if I was sure I wasn't pregnant and in the end persuaded me to see a gynaecologist. He confirmed that I was two and a half months pregnant and in danger of losing the baby if I didn't rest. Tom and I were not pleased with any of this news, it was not what we had planned and not what we wanted. I interpreted 'resting' as lying down for an hour or so in the afternoons but very soon I had a very painful miscarriage and I wondered to myself, if this is a miscarriage what on earth is a birth like? All this set us back a bit with regard to time, but eventually I was pronounced fit to continue on our travels.

In spite of the miscarriage our stay in Antwerp had been positive, Tom took a lot of pictures. He took a series of clog making in a factory near Antwerp and another in a Trappist monastery where they made beer. I was able to gain various useful pieces of information about food shopping, shortages, prices etc. and our friends, the Verschluysens, were so kind and hospitable. We headed south through the Ardennes at a leisurely pace, stopping off whenever Tom wanted to take photographs and just generally enjoying the lovely countryside in the balmy summer days.

I seem to remember that the van suffered a few mechanical problems which entailed our stopping off at various small garages and hanging around until the problem was fixed. Some nights we camped out interspersed with the odd night in a small hotel or inn when we felt in need of more comfort or better washing facilities. On the nights we camped, we always stopped much earlier because it took a while to get ourselves set up. We nearly always found some secluded spot usually near a river. We would place our camp beds at right angles to the side of the van and affix the tarpaulin to the roof rack with the other end pegged into the ground at the bottom of the beds. Thus it served as a rather inadequate tent but at least our heads and top halves were kept dry.

And so we travelled on slowly through Luxembourg and into northern France. On the whole I felt fairly OK most of the time but I did notice that I was taking a long time to dry up and now and again I was flooding. I went to consult a doctor in some French town, I forget now which, but he wasn't particularly helpful, recommended that I went to see a gynaecologist on my return to Britain and gave me a prescription for a tonic.

On we went in a leisurely way southwards through the Massif Central and the Tarn valley, often stopping off for two or three days in places which took our fancy and where there was plenty to see and photograph. Some days I felt absolutely fine and we went for long walks and climbed quite steep hills and on others I felt weak and sick and had to lie on the bed while Tom went off on his own. When we arrived at Collioure with the great Pyrenees rearing up ahead of us we had to come to a decision − to return home or to go on. We had obtained visas for Spain, with some difficulty and at considerable expense; we were loath to let them go to waste. On the other hand I did feel that my insides required some medical attention. Nowadays of course a couple like Tom and myself would have realised that I needed medical attention quite urgently and it would have been our first priority. But in those days I really hadn't much idea about my body's physical functioning and I just assumed health rather than thought about it. What could another week or ten days matter in the scheme of things? Let's go, I said and Tom was only too happy to concur.

We entered Spain at the tiny frontier town of Puigcerda. The French gendarmes told us that only seven persons had passed through there in the past six months, in fact since the frontier had been opened after the war. The Spanish Civil War had ended in April 1939, just months before the outbreak of World War II, with the defeat of the republican government, and for the next forty years Spain was to be governed by the fascist dictator, General Franco. It was not until his death that Spain made the transition to a full functioning democracy. The gendarmes were friendly and relaxed in their rather shabby and crushed uniforms. But on the Spanish side we were met by unsmiling guards in grey uniforms reminiscent of the German army. They made us take every item out of the van and lay it on the ground for inspection. At the bottom of Tom's suitcase was his Service revolver but they only riffled through the top of the case, the revolver wasn't to cause us trouble – yet. One guard disappeared with our passports and was away a long time. It had been midday when we entered Spain and baking hot; by the time we had got everything packed back in the van and our passports had been returned to us it was four o'clock. We went off in search of food and a chance to get into the shade.

We didn't really know what we would find in Spain. During the war it had been 'neutral' with a heavy bias in favour of the Axis countries. We had practically no words of Spanish other than the most basic. After we had eaten in a small and very clean restaurant, we moved away from the frontier and drove west through the most incredible mountain scenery on quite the most appalling road we had ever encountered, it was like driving on a river bed, the red, sandy surface being laced with pot holes, six inches to a foot deep. We seemed to be alone in a wilderness. Now and again we came across road making (or mending) equipment by the side of the road but little evidence that it was being put to good use and quite unexpectedly we met a bus weaving its way with great skill between the potholes. The passengers stared at us as if they had seen a *fantasma*. The van's springs had little bounce in them so we were very pleased when we arrived in a small town deep in the mountains where we found an inn which would put us up.

What surprised us pleasantly was the friendliness of the ordinary Spanish person and the cleanliness. The latter, in France, left a lot to be desired, particularly where lavatories were concerned, often only a hole in the ground in an outside shed, or if indoors, the likelihood of getting one's feet soaked when attempting to flush it. In Spain we encountered no holes in the ground and conspicuous cleanliness. It was quite a bustling little town, Seo de Urgell, where we stopped for the night and when we went out for a stroll after supper we thought we would stay for a couple of days before going on.

When he was not photographing a given series, for example, like the clogs, Tom preferred to take photos with his Leica. It was unobtrusive and people were not always conscious that they were being photographed. The following morning we went to have our breakfast in a bar and sat outside on the street watching the world go by. There were a lot of military about including *Guardia Civil* in their tricorn hats and several priests scurrying to and fro, distinctive in their black, flat hats and soutanes. Tom's camera was at the ready as we drank our coffee and he snapped away happily at faces which interested him. I noticed a couple of *guardias* on the other side of the pavement who were conferring and then one pointed across at us. "You're being watched," I said. "So?" said Tom, "let them watch."

It wasn't until we were back in the hotel that they approached us. It was after the customary late midday meal and we were sitting in the shade on the narrow little terrace of the hotel overlooking the street. They said *buenas dias señor*, that much we understood, but, not the stream of words which followed after. In despair at not being understood, the one who was doing the talking, resorted to pantomime and pointed to Tom's camera, raised his forefinger in front of his nose and waved it from side to side, at the same time shaking his head, his meaning was fairly clear and he rounded it off with a totally comprehensive – camera, no. Then they saluted and went away. And this was where we made our first mistake.

"Who do they think they are?" Tom said, "a couple of jumped-up little policemen, they needn't think I'm going to stop taking photos." I suppose, in a way, it was understandable, here were we fresh from participating in a war which had defeated Fascism and we felt ourselves to be the victors even in a country which was still Fascist and had not taken part in the war – we weren't going to be pushed around. Added to which we had no knowledge at that time of the Spanish national character which, isolated behind that vast mountain range, was supremely suspicious of foreigners, they were not to be trusted. What we also did not know and couldn't have known, was that there was considerable guerrilla activity in the mountains. Isolated groups still maintained a diminishing mini offensive against Franco's army.

I went up to our room for a lie down and Tom went off to wander about and take some more photographs. After supper we counted our money. Spain was proving quite a bit more expensive than France, there were more goods to be had and food seemed more plentiful, but you had to pay. There was a flourishing black market and those with money probably lived well. We decided that we had just about got enough money to get us back to the UK and that we ought to be making tracks and I felt it really was time that I got my insides seen to. The family who ran the hotel had been friendly at the start but after they had observed the *guardias* speaking to us they seemed more distant, but nevertheless came up with a very modest bill.

We decided it would be interesting to go back through Andorra. It was by now about mid-September and we set off on a crisp, sunny morning to go home. It took us about an hour to reach the frontier post. It was small and unimpressive, not much more than a hut at the side of the road with a few *guardias* lounging about. We assumed that they would not be that interested in us going out of the country and that it wouldn't take us long to get through. We could not have been more wrong. Once again we had to take everything out of the van and lay it along the roadside. While journeying through France Tom had developed a lot of his films en route, washing them in some convenient river or stream. They were all neatly stashed away in a box and when we had entered the country nobody had shown any interest in them. But now they were seized upon and one particularly large and coarse looking *guardia* picked up a film, which was uncut, held it up to the sun to look at it as he ran his fingers down the centre. Tom's films were like his babies before he had real ones and anyone mishandling them roused all his protective instincts and his fury. He leapt at the *guardia* and tried to wrest the film from him but was shoved roughly to one side. Meantime the *guardia* who was going through Tom's case came up with the pistol. Things didn't look too good for us.

We were made to understand that we were going to be body searched and two of the *guardia* took Tom off into their 'office' while I hung about on the road until an old woman turned up looking like a character out of one of Lorca's plays. She was dressed in black from head to toe and followed by several little urchins. Presumably she had been telephoned for because she indicated that I should follow her into a little stone shed nearby, and she drew on a pair of white cotton gloves as she went. At the entrance she turned and shoo-ed the children away who were giggling and trying to peer in. I removed my clothes, at the same time whistling rather inefficiently the Internationale which I thought was suitably defiant. The old crone paid no attention to me but carefully examined each piece of clothing as I removed it then folded it neatly and laid it on the stone bench. Then she signalled to me that I could get dressed again and left me to it.

When I emerged to rejoin Tom in the sunshine, she had disappeared and her little followers as well. We couldn't make out what was going to happen. The *cabo* or corporal was on the phone, we could see him through the open door gesticulating as he spoke. The box of developed films was on the table in front of him and the undeveloped ones they had emptied into a cloth bag. Finally he put down the phone and came out and made us understand that we should re-pack our cases and put everything back in the van. This took us a good half hour as everything was in such a jumble. But at least it seemed as if we were on our way again. When Tom indicated that he should take the films, the *guardia* shook his head and came and closed the van doors. There seemed no choice but to abandon them. Tom got into the driving seat and I got in beside him. He started the engine and we prepared to drive on until we saw two *guardias* straddling the road in front of us. One of them made a circular movement with his hand, despite our incredulity there was no mistaking his meaning, we were meant to turn around which we did, having no alternative. We then proceeded back the way we had come led by a *guardia* on a motor bike.

When we arrived back in the little town we had just left we were led by the *guardia* to the police station. There we were taken to an upstairs office where there was a civilian sitting behind a large desk smothered in papers. He asked for our passports (he had a smattering of English which was marginally better than our Spanish). He clapped the passports firmly on the desk and put his hand on top of them and then proceeded to explain to us, in as far as we could understand him, that we could not leave the country and were under house arrest until he received instructions from Madrid. This entailed going back to our original hotel in the company of a plain clothes policeman and we were installed in our original room for which we didn't have to pay.

Before we left the police station Tom asked if he could speak on the phone with the British Consul in Barcelona but this was not allowed. The staff in the hotel gave us somewhat sidelong looks but we were allowed to come and go more or less as we pleased, although always accompanied by our plump little policeman. I don't think he actually slept outside our bedroom door but he was in the reception area when we came down in the morning. Tom was allowed to go and retrieve the van from outside the police station and park it in the yard of the hotel. He locked it and hoped for the best.

This supervised existence went on for two days and then on the afternoon of the third day we were taken back to the police station where I was given back my passport and we were told that I was free to go but that Tom was to be taken under escort to Madrid, along with his films and cameras. No way was I going to be separated from my husband and I made this as clear as I could, the head policemen shrugged his shoulders and said I could go to Madrid if I wanted to but that I would have to pay my own fare. Again Tom demanded to be allowed to speak to the consul and again this was refused.

It transpired that we were to have a very early start the next morning, travelling by bus to Lérida, or Lleida as it is known today. There was only one bus a day and this left at 5.30 a.m. We packed one very small suitcase between us and left the rest of our luggage locked up in the van. We both of us went early to bed. I didn't feel too good but the next morning I felt quite a bit better as we both staggered downstairs bleary eyed to face the day. As we were drinking strong morning coffee we were introduced to Juan who was to be our new escort and accompany us to Madrid. He was young, tall and good looking and a friendly chap and Tom and he got on really well. He spoke a little English and tried to teach us bits and pieces of Spanish, he was more like an attentive host than a police escort. The three of us went out into the dark chilly morning to wait for the bus at the bus stop which wasn't far from the hotel. When it came it was already quite full, I think it had come from Pamplona, but we found seats together. Juan was carrying a big black briefcase in which were Tom's films and cameras. We didn't know what had happened to the pistol but maybe it was in his briefcase as well.

It was a bone-shaking ride but as the day dawned and the sun came up there was all this magnificent scenery to look at. The bus stopped at every tiny village, and people and livestock got on and off. At one larger village or little town Juan shot off the bus and came back with water and sandwiches for the three of us. Considering I was not under arrest, it was very generous of him to bring food for me as well. By the time we arrived in Lerida the bus was stifling hot and it was a great relief to get out. We had to traipse off to the police station but mercifully it was a short way from the bus station. Juan left us sitting in a corridor of the building while he went upstairs. He was away for a considerable time and Tom and I felt very insecure and uneasy not knowing what was going to happen and being unable to get in touch with any British official. However, eventually he came down the stairs all smiles and told us that a room had been reserved for us at an hotel as the train to Madrid did not leave until midnight. He went in search of a taxi and we drove to a small hotel. The room was small but clean and it had its own bathroom. For me it was a lifesaver as by now I was feeling very weak and tired. I lay down thankfully on the bed. Juan was going to take Tom for some lunch but I wasn't hungry so they went off on their own and I fell asleep. Two hours later they returned with a piece of *chorizo* and some fruit for me which I nibbled rather feebly. Apparently there was a circus in town and Juan had suggested we go to the first performance. I was in no state to go to a circus so I remained in the hotel room while the other two went off. They returned about an hour before we had to go to the station.

The station was seething when we got there but Juan said there was a sleeper booked for us so we felt reassured. However in reality he was unable to come up with anything, the sleeping car attendant said the sleeping car was full and our names did not figure on his list. By now there was not a seat to be had so we ended up sitting on other people's suitcases in the corridor. And so we passed an excruciatingly uncomfortable night. Not only were all the carriages full but you couldn't open the lavatory doors because of the crush of people, so in the end they remained permanently open and it was impossible to shut them. The supply of water very soon dried up and they became increasingly unhygienic. Because of my condition I had to use them, frequently, and become accustomed to not being able to shut the door. But the Spaniards are not prudish about such matters and I received kindly smiles from the women and the men looked the other way. About an hour before we reached Madrid the train emptied somewhat and we were able to find seats. Looking out of the window as the sun was rising across the arid plateau on which Madrid stands, I wondered what awaited us at the end of this nightmare journey.

Finally we arrived and soon we were in a taxi which took us to the *Puerta del Sol* where the *Guardia Civil* had its headquarters. (Decades later when I was in Madrid I went looking for the *Guardia* headquarters but it was no longer there, new offices of the electricity company had taken its place.) Juan led us into what seemed an enormous waiting room with a raised desk in the centre at which sat a *guardia*. The room was full of people moving about or sitting on benches around the walls and every now and again a name would be called out and someone would go up to the *guardia* who then wrote in the big ledger and the person either left the building or went and sat down again. Had it not been so grey and gloomy one might have imagined the *guardia* as St. Peter listening to petitions to enter heaven! Anyway, Juan deposited us on an empty bench and disappeared and that was the last we saw of him. His task was completed, he had delivered Tom and his films to the Madrid police. He had probably shot off to see his girl friend. So we sat, and we sat and we sat, a whole hour went by and nobody paid any attention to us. "Shall I go up to St. Peter and ask him what God's doing?" Tom murmured. At that moment a side door opened and another *guardia* came into the room carrying a very large key. He looked around and then came up to Tom and indicated that he was to go with him. Tom and I had a hurried embrace and I gave him our little suitcase, he would have more need of the toothpaste than me, and watched him disappear through the door with his gaoler who looked like a character out of an opera with that outsize key.

Now what? I was not under arrest and had no need to remain any longer in that dismal waiting room. But I sat down again on the bench in order to collect my thoughts and count my money. Tom had turned over all our spare cash to me, keeping only a few pesetas. Obviously my first course of action was to go to the British Embassy to seek help. I emerged from the police building on to the sunny street and became acutely aware that I couldn't string a sentence together in Spanish. But hailing a taxi is much the same anywhere and the driver seemed to know where the British Embassy was. I entered a leafy front courtyard and up imposing steps, so different from the building I had just left. The receptionist was Spanish and spoke excellent English so communication was no problem. I outlined our plight and asked to see someone who could help. She got on the internal phone and a few minutes later a plump, middle-aged man appeared in the hall and took me into an office.

I must have looked a terrible sight, unkempt, crumpled and probably none too clean, besides which I was feeling like death and I presumed it showed. When I had finished recounting what had happened, (and I did also sketch in my medical problem), instead of some friendly comforting response, I was subjected to a five minute long harangue on the stupidity of British tourists' behaviour in a Fascist country where you do what you're told, and avoid the trouble caused thereby to the embassy. I felt like bursting into tears. I had forgotten, or not taken in that it was a Saturday and of course nearly all the embassy personnel had gone out of town for the weekend. There was nothing to be done he said about getting Tom out of gaol until the Monday when the embassy would be back in business and it would probably take several days. He then relented somewhat and asked me whether I had anywhere to stay and when I said no, we went to the reception and he asked Carmen to ring around some hotels for me.

"You look exhausted," she said when he had disappeared. "Sit down and I'll get you some coffee." She came back with a cup of milky coffee and a plate of biscuits. I sat and drank it gratefully while she rang up one or two hotels. Somewhere modest, I told her, I haven't got much money. Before long she found me a room and wrote down the name and address of the hotel in large, clear script and then she telephoned for a taxi. She came to the front door with me and as we said goodbye she put her arm round my shoulder and said – good luck. I felt it was somewhat ironic that the only support and comfort I received at the British Embassy was from the Spanish receptionist. Well, I thought indignantly, they've been sitting on their backsides in a cushy billet for so long, they're out of touch with the real world.

The hotel was fine, on the fourth floor but there was a lift. The room had two beds and there was an en suite bathroom. I had a shower and fell into bed and slept for most of the day. I awoke in the late afternoon and ventured out to buy a toothbrush and toothpaste. It was far too early to eat in any restaurant and anyway I wasn't keen to brave one on my own so I had a sandwich and a *horchata* sitting out on the street at a cafe near the hotel. I returned to my room and went back to bed again, mercifully I had a book with me.

Somehow I got through the weekend and awoke on Monday morning with a sense of anticipation. But the day passed without anything happening. In the early evening I got the hotel to put through a call to the Embassy. Be patient, I was told, we're doing our best. And so I went to bed for a third night on my own. I was in a deep sleep when the phone beside my bed rang. It was the night porter – "I have a gentleman here, señora, who says he's your husband." I could hardly believe my ears and within minutes Tom came into the room. We fell into each other's arms. He too had been awakened from sleep, by a guard who told him he was released but was to report every day to the police station while his films were being developed and assessed. He asked if he could finish his sleep and leave in the morning. But no, they had received the order for his release, he was free, he must go now. So there was nothing for it but to get dressed, collect up his few belongings and leave. There were few taxis around at that hour but eventually one did come along and he instructed the driver to take him to an hotel. He had no idea where I was lodged so it was pure chance and marvellous good luck that he ended up at the same hotel!

After the first euphoria of reunion had passed, we sat down the following morning at a cafe table to take stock of our situation and – yes – to count our money. No way were we going to get back to the UK with the money in our pockets and we had no idea how much longer we would have to remain in Madrid, that depended on the Spanish police. Our traveller's cheques had been all cashed and these were pre-credit card days. Cabled money took days rather than hours to arrive. We decided to send a telegram to my parents and Tom's brother Wilfred and let them know what had happened to us. Curiously enough the police had returned Tom's cameras to him after removing the film so he loaded them up again (his unused films had been returned to him) and as we strolled in the Retiro park he photographed the nursemaids and their charges, solid looking women with their distinctive three ball ear rings which were the insignia of their occupation. Nobody, neither police nor public paid him any attention so he went on to photograph other things.

On our second day together I felt unbearably hot – no it was not any hotter than usual, Tom told me when I questioned him. That night I slept fitfully and when I woke up I was very damp and very hot and I saw that the red pyjamas I was wearing had dyed the white sheets a pale pink. I did not feel like getting out of bed and Tom asked the hotel to call a doctor. We had to wait several hours but eventually he came. When he took my temperature it was 104. He spoke a little English and I told him about my miscarriage in Antwerp and subsequent problems on the journey to Madrid. He immediately said that he would send a gynaecologist to examine me. The gynaecologist arrived within half an hour, took one look at me and said that I must be hospitalised immediately and recommended the Anglo-American hospital. He also asked the hotel for an ice bag which he put on my stomach. "You have an inflammatory infection," he told me. He said he would ring the hospital and a nurse would come to accompany me there. He spoke very good English and remained my doctor until I left Spain. Left alone again, Tom and I held hands in scared silence.

It was during my sojourn at the Anglo-American hospital that I had my second brush with death although I did not realise it at the time. It was a clinic rather than a hospital from the point of view of size. The matron was English, trained at Barts and such a nice woman, she lent Tom money when his supply dried up and never reproached him. The nurses were Spanish and French and there was an English sister who came from St. Thomas's. The main drift of my treatment was to reduce the infection and bring my temperature down. But I did not respond and my fever increased. I was given M and B, that ubiquitous drug that we came to know so well during the war, but it had no effect. There was no penicillin in Spain in 1946, at least not for general public use. I well remember the rigors I had as my condition grew worse. I could feel my temperature going up like an elevator and then suddenly I would be drenched in sweat and start to shake and shiver and get colder and colder as blankets were heaped on top of me until the shaking gradually tapered off and, exhausted, I would fall into shallow sleep.

This went on for several days, I forget how many, and it usually happened in the early evening. I think it was my capacity to sweat so profusely that contributed to my recovery, that and of course, far more, the penicillin Matron finally acquired from the Embassy. There was one little French nurse who looked after me. She was sweet but her emotions always broke through any professional front she possessed. I always knew when my temperature had gone up because she ran from my room waving the thermometer above her head. On this particular morning she not only ran from the room but called desperately for Sister. Many weeks later, when I was in St. Thomas's and managed to sneak a look at my notes, I read that on this particular morning my temperature had gone up to 107. It was from then on that I started to have penicillin injections, every three hours, twenty-four hours a day. It had become clear that the Spanish available drugs were having no effect on my condition and after conferring with my doctor, Matron got in touch with the British Embassy who had a supply of penicillin.

It was a day or two before I started responding, but gradually the rigors stopped and my temperature came down. The aim was to get me sufficiently stable to be able to be airlifted back to hospital in Britain because every day spent in Spain was a drain on our non-existent financial resources. Matron had contacts at St. Thomas's with whom she had been in touch on the phone and she assured me that a bed had been reserved for me there.

Tom visited me every day. By great good luck he had bumped into a young chap we had known in Cairo who was now living in Madrid and he offered Tom floor space and a mattress, so he was not having to pay for an hotel any longer. By now those at home were aware of what had happened and my father cabled Tom £50. I encouraged him to visit at lunchtime so that he could eat some of my enormous midday meal which I barely touched. I was fed three square meals a day, an English cooked breakfast, a Spanish three-course lunch and a more modest supper. The midday meal was always topped off with about half a kilo of grapes and it was literally years before I could face grapes again. Even now I only like very small bunches.

Tom reported every morning to the police but could not find out how long it was going to take to develop all the films and assess them. Of course they were nearly all of France and Belgium and only a very small percentage had been taken in Spain, but that cut no ice with the *guardias*. It was on one of his early visits that Tom sat by my bed and held my hand – "Darling, darling, please don't die," he said and I can remember thinking, he's over emotional, as I told him I had no intention of dying. It wasn't until just before I left for Britain and Sister was sitting on my bed chatting and she said, "I hope you'll never be so ill again," that I realised what a close haul I'd had.

The penicillin injections were highly unpleasant, the Spaniards used needles like you would inject a horse with and when the penicillin went in, it bit down my leg so I would roll over and bite my pillow to stop myself crying out. The little French nurse was very bad at giving them, she was too gentle and when the needle was half way in she had to give it a push. I much preferred the Spanish nurse who whammed the needle home with a hearty punch. I remember one night when the French nurse came in to give me my 3 a.m. injection and I was lying quietly with my eyes closed though not asleep, I opened them and saw her peering at me in the semi darkness. I moved to roll over and present my pin-cushion like bottom when she clapped her free hand against her chest and exclaimed – *"Je crois vous êtes morte." "Pas encore,"* came my reply as I steeled myself for the puncture! Gradually I stabilised and once my temperature had come down to 102 I was deemed fit to travel to the UK. I must have been a weird sight as I travelled dressed in pyjamas and wrapped in blankets. I was carried down to the taxi and Tom and Sister accompanied me to the airport. The other passengers were all in their seats when I was carried aboard and laid on two empty seats at the back of the aircraft. Tom had bought me a large amount of fresh fruit which was contained in a string bag and placed in the overhead locker. It was terrible saying goodbye to him because we did not know when we would see one another again and when the aircraft took off, I had a quiet little weep. We landed at Toulouse for refuelling and the other passengers got off for half an hour or so. The steward, who was a big, friendly Aberdonian, came to see how I was getting on and when I told him I needed to go to the lavatory he picked me up and dumped me on the toilet – no bother. Then he brought me a cup of tea. When we arrived at Heathrow, there was an ambulance on the tarmac waiting for me. I was transferred to this by the steward, plus my bag of fruit, before the rest of the passengers disembarked.

I don't think I've ever been so glad to return to Britain, either before or since, and as the ambulance sped towards central London and I could see out of the small windows in the ambulance, the grey sky of a dull October day, I felt I had come home. When we reached St. Thomas's hospital they put me in a wheelchair, with my fruit on my lap and a porter wheeled me up to the ward. When he handed me over to the ward Sister, his cockney wit came to the fore – "'ere's your patient, Sister, and 'alf of Covent Garden too."

I was just over three weeks in St. Thomas's. They continued the penicillin treatment for another five days, but oh the difference! The needles used were many sizes smaller than the Spanish ones and the nurses were quiet, efficient and reassuring. My mother came down from Edinburgh and visited me every day, she stayed with Francis' mother-in-law at Roehampton. Eventually I had a letter from Tom. He had been freed and his films returned but developed and damaged. He had had to borrow money from the Embassy to pay the hospital bill and to get him home and when he arrived in England his passport was impounded until such time as he repaid his debt to the Foreign Office. He travelled north to collect the van and found it with flat tyres and broken into. One or two of our belongings had been removed including my new expensive mac. In Andorra he ran into a terrible snow blizzard and then the foot brake failed and he had to drive all the way to Paris on the hand brake before he could get it fixed. The final blow came the night he landed in Newhaven and had gone to his parents' home in Iver, Buckinghamshire – his mother, who was in hospital with heart trouble, died before Tom was able to visit her.

Once my temperature became normal I had a curettage and an incredible amount of rubbish was removed from my insides. I have a theory which may or may not be correct, that because twins were in the Robson family, I had been pregnant with twins and at the time of the miscarriage one foetus came away while the other remained and became infected causing the septicaemia which made me so ill. On his second day home Tom came to London to visit me and we filled each other in with all that had happened to us since we parted. Tom's immediate task was to try and set up evening photographic classes at Epsom Art School where the lack of equipment and the post-war difficulties of getting anything done were to prove endlessly frustrating to him.

I was by now ready to move on. I was still very weak and underweight, barely 7 stone and I went back to Edinburgh with my mother for a prolonged convalescence under the parental roof. Dr Flett came to give me the once over and said that I must have a very strong constitution to have survived. He recommended rest, fresh air, good food and the occasional glass of champagne.

Tom and I were not to see each other again until Christmas. We had no home and practically no money and debts to my father and the Foreign Office. So Tom had to live with his bereaved father and his brother Wilfred in the small, very inconvenient Iver house and battle away on his own without me. He got some money together from published articles and photographs and so with that and his small Surrey county council salary for Epsom, he was able to pay my father back and enjoy Christmas spent with my family in Edinburgh. After Christmas I returned with Tom to Iver and so I came to look after the three male Weedons (my father-in-law suffered a very small stroke so he needed extra care) throughout that bitter, bitter winter of forty-seven.

It was not an easy household to manage, Tom and Wilfred were often at loggerheads and it didn't improve matters that Tom sometimes converted the inconvenient little kitchen into a dark room just when Wilfred wanted to cook. Old Mr Weedon would become distressed when the boys or I did not do things as he would have liked them to be done. He had been a great stickler for domestic precision and order and he was frustrated that he could no longer undertake certain jobs himself. Tom and I never seemed to be on our own except in bed and the nights were much too short. All this was compounded by the appalling weather and the hazardous car journeys both Wilfred and Tom had to make to their respective places of work. One evening on the way home from Kingston Wilfred's car overturned but he was mercifully unhurt.

But eventually spring came and the thaw set in. Tom and I began to look for somewhere to live. It was quite a disheartening process, we even considered a converted assault boat on the river at Twickenham. But at long last, in the early summer, we moved into a home of our own – Monks Hatch, on the Hogs Back, near Guildford.

There you have it, David, your grandparents' disastrous journey to Spain. I was always surprised that it didn't prejudice us when we came to buy the house in Fornalutx because in the fifties all foreigners buying houses had to have clearance from Madrid. We awaited the reply to our application with bated breath, but I suppose in those days computers were not in general use and the Spanish authorities were neither efficient nor organised, so Tom did not figure as a *persona non grata*.

Much love to you both and my little great-granddaughter,

Veronica

Veronica and Priscilla

Frank and Priscilla

Elizabeth, Francis, Priscilla and Veronica

Summer holidays - Bella, Veronica, Elizabeth, Francis

Veronica and father at Croftmore

Holiday in Mull with one of the Livingston brothers

Lettoch near Nethy Bridge. Our first car.

Lindhu, Isle of Mull, holidays with the Colvin family

Summer - Isle of Mull, Priscilla, Veronica, Aunt Sophie, Elizabeth,
Uncle Hugh, Aunt Totty

Germany – Ursula and Veronica

July 1939 – visiting Elizabeth on open day at Red Cross VAD
camp in Fife

Dalmeny – Veronica and Eve with transport mates

Cairo Heliopolis, the museum

Baalbeck

Baalbeck – with Fawzi

Sinai

Sinai – en route to St Catherine's Monastery

Sinai, El Tor

Italy, Conversano – with Signor Rutigliano and Pep

Bletchley

London, Hyde Park

January 1946 – London, Chelsea – after our wedding

London, Handel Street

Camping in Belgium

Brussels

Monk's Hatch

Cedar Cottage

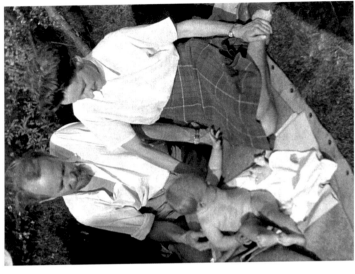

Camping in the Dordogne
(Cordelia's first foreign holiday)

At Glyndebourne, Wilfred Veronica and Tom

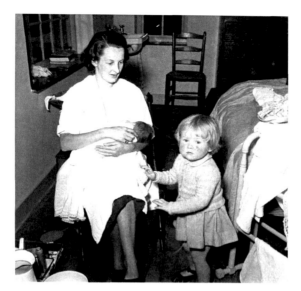

Veronica, Tom Simon and Cordelia

Cedar Cottage – Veronica and Cordelia

Shortly after Fiona was born, 1954

Martin, Cordelia, Tom Simon and Fiona

The tree house – Cedar Cottage

1956 – Fornalutx –Tom Simon, Martin, Veronica and Cordelia

View of Fornalutx

Mallorca

1957 – Fornalutx – our house

1962 – Veronica at Sa Pedruscada

Sa Pedruscada

Family at Sa Pedruscada

1963 – Christmas at Cedar Cottage with our neighbours, the Uptons

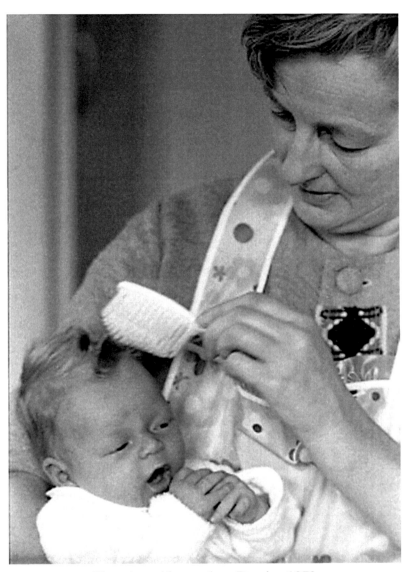

Veronica with grandson Damian 1973

1980 – Veronica at Bolt Cottage

Dearest Jason

I still find it difficult to think of you in faraway Chicago, your Mum tells me that you are moving from your apartment into a house. I've had a few moves in my lifetime. The biggest and most complicated, of course, was our move out to Fornalutx from Cedar Cottage in the early summer of 1959. Then the move back in 1962 – that I think was the most traumatic – back to Cedar Cottage which not only was full of ghosts and memories from the past but was also a house trashed by uncaring tenants so that almost nothing in the house worked. But the most physically difficult move was from Monks Hatch to Cedar Cottage.

In Monks Hatch we had plenty of space, good sized rooms which coped with quite large pieces of furniture, no problem. By comparison Cedar Cottage was like a matchbox and we couldn't get our bed up the stairs. It had to be sent away to be sawn in half and hinged so that it could be manoeuvred into the house. Tom and I slept on the floor for weeks before the bed was finally installed. But if the house seemed tiny compared to where we had come from, we had great space outside, two and a half acres of woodland and from the top of a tall oak tree, you could see Box Hill, near Dorking. On the day of our arrival, Tom spent the evening hammering in the iron pegs he had bought to make a ladder up the tree. I did think to myself that he might have been more usefully employed giving me a hand and doing some hammering *inside* the house! But he was like an excited schoolboy when he came to tell me he had reached the top of the tree so I hadn't the heart to dampen his enthusiasm. He often shinned up that tree but I have to admit that I never got more than halfway up, it was too high above the ground for my liking.

Cedar Cottage was about a mile and a half from the village of Newdigate in Surrey. It was on a private road, in other words a rutted lane full of potholes. Once a year, we residents turned out to give it a day's labour, filling in the potholes with small stones and cinders and leavening the bumps with whatever tools we could lay our hands on, but the 'repairs' never lasted for long. None of us wanted to pay out the money required to have it professionally repaired and tarmaced. Anyway it was quite a jolly social event, cheered on by the odd glass of beer.

There were about six other houses tucked away in the woods and we all knew one another to a greater or lesser extent. But it was the Uptons, Denis and Zoë and their daughter Ann, who were our closest friends in Ewood Lane, as it was called. Ann was more or less the same age as Cordelia and they grew up together, being great pals in their childhood and getting up to all sorts of pranks. Their ways began to diverge in their teens and in adulthood there was not a lot left. Ann married a missionary doctor and emigrated to Canada. Denis and Zoë were an unfailing source of help and support in many of those minor domestic crises which blow up in the course of family life. We didn't live in each other's pockets by any means, weeks would go by without our even catching a glimpse of one another, but they were *there* and dependable. It was not that we had outlooks in common, in fact Tom and I couldn't have been more different really. They were politically Conservative and the epitome of conventionality, at least outwardly, although I think there were problems beneath the surface, but we were mutually tolerant and I shall always remember them with affection. Sadly Zoë was killed in a car accident shortly after our return from Fornalutx. Denis had a sad and difficult final period of life and died in his mid sixties.

So Cedar Cottage was where the rest of our four children were born and spent their early years. Both your uncle Tom and your mum were actually born in the house and I have to say that she – Fiona – was my only 'pretty' baby, like a little rosebud. But I am leaping ahead of time. At the time of our move – June 1949 – there were just the three of us. It didn't take long to settle in after the initial shock of moving into somewhere so much smaller. We were all set to go to France at the end of July. Cordelia started on foreign travel at a year old, tucked up in her Moses basket on the back seat of our 'new' car. We didn't see any reason for not going on our travels just because we had a baby. True we made one or two concessions to making our travelling conditions a little less spartan. We got rid of our Morris van which had carried us so many miles and bought a Morris saloon with broad running boards. It looked quite grand but the engine was not in keeping with its appearance and gave us considerable trouble. We also bought a proper tent to replace the old tarpaulin which had previously given us rather inadequate shelter. France had always been Tom's first love and he would have liked to buy a house there had we been able to afford it.

This summer we were heading for the Dordogne. Friends were coming to stay in the house while we were gone and they arrived the evening of our departure. Sid Matthews was head of the photography department of Ealing Art College and Tom had done some part-time teaching there. He was a technical chap and it was the technical side of photography rather than creative perception which interested him. He and his wife and their small son Michael lived in Surbiton and so were not averse to a week or two in the country. I had planned our departure (or so I thought) so that it would not interrupt Cordelia's routine. We were to leave around 6 p.m. when she would have been fed and ready for sleep as we drove down to the Channel port where we were staying the night. However Tom suddenly remembered he had forgotten to select the photographs which he wanted to submit to the Royal Photographic Society's annual exhibition and as they would have to be sent off immediately on our return, he wanted to sort them out before we left. So we set off a good three hours later than planned. If you marry a creative spirit you have to be prepared to be flexible!

We had a very happy holiday camped on the banks of the Dordogne, not far from the market town of Sarlat and quite near the Chateau de Montfort of which Tom took many photographs, both then and in subsequent years when we were travelling south to Barcelona. We would push Cordelia in her pushchair to Sarlat where we shopped and quite often had lunch. She was no trouble and was mostly smiley and happy. She slept at night in a folding pram we had brought and we used the pushchair for walks. It was all very peaceful and rural and I washed the nappies in the river and dried them, weighted down by stones, on the river bank. Cordelia crawled on the soft grass and made sporadic efforts to get on her feet. Tom took lots of photographs and we drank plenty good red wine. It was the days when France was plastered with billboards which read – *un repas sans vin c'est comme un jour sans soleil.* I seem to remember Tom dipping his finger into his wineglass and offering it to Cordelia to suck. It was mostly cloudless blue skies and very warm without being oppressive but one night we had an almighty storm of wind, thunder and lightning. Tucked up in her pram, Cordelia slept through it unconcernedly while Tom and I quaked in our double sleeping bag waiting for disaster to strike. It didn't. After ten days we reluctantly turned our faces north again and had an uneventful journey home apart from the fact that the radiator leaked and the engine overheated. Decades later, when I was staying with Tom and Sue in a house they had rented on the Dordogne, I tried to identify the bend in the river where we had camped but I could not – it was all so changed.

And so the rest of the children all arrived at two yearly intervals. The first was Tom whom we called Tom Simon to differentiate him from his father, and who scared us for the first few days because he was so jaundiced. I had what was then known as a monthly nurse, i.e. a nurse who attended you at the birth and stayed on afterwards to help look after the baby for a week or two.

We did not know this, but apparently some months previously she had had a baby die on her who had been very jaundiced and so she was in a highly nervous state with Tom Simon and spent most of her time in the kitchen making jam to calm her nerves. Both Tom and I got very irritated with her and were much relieved when she left. Tom Simon's jaundice soon abated and he flourished. The next one to come along, two months before expected, was Martin, in the icy, foggy month of November 1952. His arrival really threw a spanner in the family works. I was whisked off to hospital, leaving Tom, who was feeling miserable with sinusitis, to look after two clamorous small children with the doubtful help of a sullen French au pair girl who seemed not remotely interested in the children. Friends and neighbours were as helpful as they could be but it was one of those winters when everyone's children seemed to have ailments or else their parents were ill so there was not that much help around. In the end, my mother, your great-grandmother, Priscilla, offered to have them and someone was found to take Cordelia and Tom Simon up to Edinburgh by train. My mother said that they arrived looking like waifs out of a storm. By now Tom had developed quite a nasty dose of flu and went to stay with his brother, Wilfred who had a flat in East Molesey. The French girl went back to France and Cedar Cottage closed down for a week or two.

On reflection, I think it was quite something for my mother, who always had nannies and maids to help her, to undertake the care of two young children on her own, in her small and spotless flat. Luckily my brother Francis and his wife Diana lived not far away so she did have some respite. Now that I was relieved of extraneous anxieties, I could get on with the job on hand. Martin had taken a long time to get born. It was as if he had thought better of his initial rush towards the world and wanted to stay warm and protected a little longer. But he eventually emerged, weighing 4 lbs. and was immediately put into an incubator. The nurses loved him and called him Timmy as they fed him with my expressed milk from a pipette. It was a month before he was strong enough to feed himself. Owing to the weather I had no visitors and when visiting time came round I felt a bit miserable, most of the other mums came from Dorking so their husbands and families hadn't far to come. Wilfred attempted to bring Tom down one evening but they had to turn back because of fog and black ice. I spent five weeks in hospital, until Martin weighed 5 lbs. and was strong enough for me to be allowed to take him home. Wilfred went to Edinburgh and brought the other two back so finally we were all happily re-united again.

Twenty months later, in early July 1954, came Fiona. She wasn't expected for another month and I was in my vegetable garden staking green beans. Tom had gone off to London for the day on some photographic project and didn't expect to be home until late in the evening. I thought I felt a contraction but dismissed it as imagination. However I was soon unable to ignore them and I rang the district nurse who said to have a bath and get into bed and she would be with me shortly. Fortunately this was the time when we had our best au pair, a German girl called Christel who was devoted to the children and totally reliable. I told her what was happening and then retired to bed with a book.

When the district nurse arrived she very soon phoned the doctor but by the time he arrived it was all done and dusted. Fiona weighed only four and a half pounds but did not look the least bit premature. The cradle was still up in the loft so she started off life tucked up in a drawer. Christel brought the children in to view the new arrival. They peered into the drawer, kissed me goodnight and went off to bed without comment. I suppose they were used to being a group and this one was just another addition. Not like when Tom Simon was born to put Cordelia's nose out of joint and I found sand from the sand pit all over his face as he lay asleep in his pram. "Baby cubberd i'sand" was her comment which perhaps showed an unconscious desire on Cordelia's part for baby to be obliterated. Still, it had none of the passion of my own brother's reputed behaviour when I was born. He allegedly battered on my parents' bedroom door and sobbed – "send her back, send her back." He already had one bossy sister and he longed for a brother. I was never quite sure whether this was an apocryphal tale or not, but quite recently I was reading my mother's diary of the year in which I was born and on the day of my birth, after eulogies to the new baby, my mother wrote – "Francis wept."

When Tom came home that night he found the Rayburn stove in the kitchen had been riddled and stoked by our departing doctor, his one contribution to the birth. Upstairs I was in bed with our new daughter asleep in a drawer. Tom was a bit disappointed as he had wanted to photograph her birth, but photographers can't always be in the right place at the right time! On reflection, I think I got the greatest early babyhood pleasures from my first born and my last. With Cordelia I had no other demands and once I had fed her, I often used to walk about the room with her in my arms until she fell asleep. Then also I had such a lovely monthly nurse after I came out of hospital. I had known her since my childhood – Miss Mac or Tookie as we used to call her. She had been governess to my cousins Sheila and Betty More, a soft spoken west Highlander from one of the Outer Isles, who could turn her hand to anything and had a wonderful sense of humour. When Sheila and Betty outgrew her, she went off to train as a nurse and took up midwifery. She brought several of my sister Bud's children into the world. Of course when Fiona arrived I was already an old hand, and her birth was so easy and she herself so serene and content. It wasn't until she was a toddler that her more volatile temperament became apparent.

It was not that I did not enjoy the boys' babyhood but their early weeks were not so peaceful and in Martin's case positively fraught. I had to feed him every three hours, then test weigh him and if he hadn't taken enough, express my milk and give him the rest in a bottle. It seemed as if I had no sooner laid him down from one feed then it was time to pick him up and start another. Then I got a nasty dose of flu which dragged me down. Somewhat reluctantly I stopped breast feeding and felt a thousand times better. It was curious that my babies got progressively smaller but no one seemed to take much interest. Pre-natal care was fairly perfunctory in my day, your blood pressure was monitored, your stomach poked about, but unless you displayed any obvious negative symptoms, that was about it. No ecographs, scans and all that jazz like nowadays! But I suppose I was really very lucky to have had children after what happened to me in Madrid.

Family life at Cedar Cottage proceeded happily and settled down to a steady rhythm of homemaking and child rearing. We cleared a lot of the ground round the house and made a rough garden which could withstand the depredations of vigorous children. Tom built them a tree house between three strategically placed oaks, he put wooden pegs into one of the trees for them to climb up into the house and rigged up a rubber tyre on a steel cable which descended to the ground from the tree house. It was a good thing they had a father who encouraged them to climb, to swing and to balance because I was physically very unadventurous and invariably foresaw disaster. But the children were fearless and agile, they were taught to climb safely and we never had an accident. Just as they used to scamper up the steps here in Fornalutx to the very top terrace without the safety of a railing. (The present railing is an addition in my retirement for safety in old age!)

We had a dog called Mungo, a series of cats, hens, rabbits and for a short while two very nasty geese. They got eaten for Christmas. We did not go out on excursions much because there always seemed so much to do at home. When they were old enough, Tom would take Cordelia and Tom Simon to London, to museums, to the zoo or just around with him while he took photographs, but for the most part we had plenty of ploys at home. At the weekends we nearly always had visitors, especially in the summer. We were sitting ducks really, people just used to drive in at the gate unannounced. We soon changed from politely stopping what we were doing and entertaining them. Uninvited guests were immediately co-opted into the job on hand, were it mixing concrete or chopping down a tree. If that wasn't to their taste, another job was found for them or they just had to hang around, watching. Invited guests were treated with more consideration.

There was no form of pre-school education anywhere near us and none of our children had any. When I see today's young children occupied with a multiplicity of organised activities with scarcely a free moment, I wonder whether ours were hard done by. On the other hand they had a wonderfully free and unrestricted pre-school period. There were other children down the lane and they all played (and squabbled) together. Mostly they seemed to congregate on our land and in the woods were endless camps and hideouts, partially damned ditches and makeshift fences. Activities arose out of their own imaginations and their games were made up or improvised by themselves. Apart from 'cowboys and Indians' they had no stereotyped models. But school came as a nasty shock, particularly for poor Cordelia who was the first to absorb it, and on her first day she cried almost the entire time.

My father died during this time, in January 1951, he was 72. He had undergone an operation, not a very serious one, and had returned home but some complication set in and when my mother phoned me from Edinburgh I could not quite believe it. It was my first meaningful encounter with death. I left Tom in charge of Cordelia and took Tom Simon with me to Edinburgh for two or three days. That first evening in Edinburgh I had to go into my parents' bedroom for something and I was brought up short when I was faced with my father's coffin, placed on trestles. Somehow I did not expect him to be still in the house For a moment I was frozen to the spot The coffin lid was closed. Then I advanced into the room towards it and gingerly raised the lid a few inches. I caught a last glimpse of my father's face, in death. I was unaware at the time, how later on, I would become accustomed to looking at the dead in houses here in Fornalutx, which I visited to offer condolences.

Some months before Fiona was born Tom's work took a change of direction. Freelancing was all very well but it was erratic and cheques were slow in coming in. He taught evening classes at Epsom and Guildford but no money from that came in during the holidays. The house in Iver, where Tom's parents had lived, was now let to members of the American forces. Tom's share of that came directly to my account for the housekeeping. Occasionally Wilfred was dilatory about sending the cheque and I would be jumping up and down, having to shop on credit. With the family getting bigger, our outgoings increased and when Tom was offered the full-time job of Senior Lecturer at Guildford Art College, it seemed like a heaven sent gift – a regular monthly cheque, twelve months a year.

At first Tom was worried about losing his freedom and being unable to do his own work, but they came to a happy compromise, he would work four days a week for Guildford and one day for himself. Thus he could still be a practising photographer and bring his experience of this into his teaching. I had been so used to Tom working from home, that it seemed quite strange at first having him 'go out' to work and I missed him. But in the long run it made it easier to organize the day. What I didn't miss was the juggling of the bills each month, deciding which could wait and which simply *had* to be paid. We always had car repair bills but our garage was very patient and it wasn't until they stuck their purple label with PLEASE written on it, at the foot of the bill, that I knew we could delay payment no longer. The coal man always had to wait until the summer. But now the bills could be paid in a less idiosyncratic manner.

The event which was to change all our lives so sadly had not yet cast the first, faint shadow across our existence. We lived in a happy and fulfilled present, mercifully ignorant of the future. Towards the end of the war, when he was stationed in Antwerp, the building where his unit was housed received a direct hit from a V2 (a radar guided powerful flying missile, heir to the V1, the buzz bomb). Tom was buried for twelve hours and when they dug him out he had to be operated on to remove glass from his brain and also his right hand and arm suffered from being bent beneath his body for all that time. For these injuries he received a small pension and periodically had to appear before a pensions board. He went for one, the autumn after Fiona was born and they told him that albumen had been detected in his urine and that he should go and see his own doctor. Our doctor referred him to the hospital and the consultant there diagnosed nephritis. Neither of us had heard of nephritis and we were told that it was an inflammation of the kidneys as the result of permanent damage. In Tom's case this was possibly brought about by the quantities of M and B which had been given to him during various wartime hospitalisations, especially in Egypt, without consuming sufficient fluids to flush it out of the kidneys. Tom was told that there was nothing that could be done about it, medically speaking. He was advised to reduce his salt intake, to cut out spirits and only drink wine in small quantities, also to avoid possible throat infections. Apart from that he was to continue to lead a normal life. Almost as an afterthought it was added that this condition would of course curtail his life expectancy and that he was unlikely to live much beyond his late sixties. He was then 45 and I was 35. As you may imagine, Jason, a cold draught blew in under our door, but it was quickly sucked out again by the thought that Tom's sixties had not yet appeared on the horizon and anything could happen between now and then.

Apart from observing the precautions advised, we decided to put it out of our minds as much as possible. We both of us lived very much in the here and now and life was positive and happy. Tom's work was going well. He had established himself in the photographic world and was often in demand to judge professional exhibitions and competitions. His own work was being published in France and America as well as in Britain. The monthly cheque from Guildford was a great ease to our financial situation, and so life rolled on.

By the time Fiona was a year old we had planned another trip abroad and were going to take Cordelia, aged 7 and Tom Simon, aged 5, with us. Martin and Fiona were being left with Christel in whom we had implicit faith. She had been with us for eighteen months and had a really good relationship with all the children. She was not worried at being left in charge and she had our friends, the Uptons, down the lane as back-up. We had rented a flat over a village shop on the shores of Lake Lucerne in Switzerland. Off we set, no mobile phones, no email, just post for communication and, in emergencies, telegrams or long distance phone calls. Happily there were no emergencies and Christel sent me twice weekly, long letters detailing Martin and Fiona's daily doings, the state of their health and appetite and Martin's latest sayings.

It must seem very strange to you, Jason, to live in a world without instant communication, but what we didn't have we didn't miss. Instant communication is undoubtedly a wonderful and highly useful invention but it means, in a sense, that the umbilical cord is never cut. We can always be in contact with someone somewhere by pushing a button and maybe, just maybe, the quality of communication is poorer than when we had to make more effort. Anyway, to continue with our holiday, the four of us waved goodbye to the two little ones and set off for Switzerland.

After a series of rather bad buys, we now had a much newer 'new' car – a Singer Gazelle, a snazzy little sports type car with a silver body and red leather seats. It was fun to drive and never gave us any problems but there wasn't a lot of room in the back. On the way, we camped at night and reached our destination on the fourth day Apart from asking at frequent intervals – are we there yet? – the two children were pretty good travellers. They invented their own noisy games, one of which consisted of being a radio and belting out songs like

Davy Crockett, King of the Wild Frontier. They had a 'volume button' which they 'tuned' to minimum, then full volume. I tried to introduce more educational games, requiring some mental effort but they only entered these half heartedly and soon reverted to their own inventions. From time to time they slept, to the infinite relief of their parents, especially the one who was at the wheel!

It was a good holiday on the whole, the flat was simple but light and airy and our landlords, who were the shopkeepers, were friendly and helpful. Tom had just acquired a cine camera and we also brought with us a portable recorder and for the first time recorded sounds to go with the pictures and the cine film. Wherever we went we lugged this heavy, clumsy machine with us but its quality of sound was good. The most interesting thing we recorded was a farmer blowing this enormous horn on the hillside – not a melodious sound, but extraordinary. We walked, we went for trips on the lake, up funiculars, and once across a small iceberg. The children for a joke locked Tom and myself in the kitchen and then panicked when they couldn't turn the key to let us out. Whenever we were in need of butter, Tom Simon would go down to the shop, muttering his carefully rehearsed phrase – *hundert gram butter bitte.*

For part of the time we had two friends staying with us. Peter was a keen photographer and went to Tom's evening classes at Epsom. He was Viennese and Sylvia, his companion, was Czech, a strikingly beautiful woman, who had a little boy, Charles, by a previous marriage. They lived in Peter's mother's large house in Leatherhead, together with his sister who was as large and extrovert as Peter was small and excessively reserved. He ran a glove business in London, importing the gloves from Vienna. His sister was an impresario and there were often celebrated musicians staying in the house. That was where Tom photographed the singer, Hans Hotter. Charles was between Cordelia and Tom Simon in age and the three of them played happily together.

With two sets of parents available, it meant we could go off for a few days on our own. Peter and Sylvia went first and we looked after Charles, and then it was our turn. We went into Italy for a couple of days. We were always hopeful that we might find a house one day in the sun which we could afford to buy and use for summer holidays. We both yearned for the sun and didn't take kindly to the British climate after our war service in Egypt, and subsequent travels.

We stayed overnight at Lake Orta and there on the edge of that enchanting little lake was a turreted house for sale. It was large and furnished and as we wandered through the well proportioned rooms and looked out of the windows across the lake, it laid a considerable spell on us. But it cost the equivalent of two thousand pounds and we did not have that sort of money. The only possible way we could buy that house would have been to sell up in England and move to Italy. We sat for a long time on an upturned boat on the lakeside and considered this possibility. But there was too much at stake. As parents of four children, we felt it would be irresponsible to uproot them and drag them along in the wake of our particular whim. Also Tom was enjoying his work at Guildford and we were both enjoying greater financial security which would have to be built up all over again if we moved to Italy. So regretfully, but quite decisively, we rejected the idea. Subsequently I heard that Lake Orta, like so many places, has become massively developed as a tourist resort and so obviously has lost much of its charm.

We returned to our Swiss holiday. Switzerland, on the whole, did not appeal greatly to us as a country in spite of its many virtues. It seemed so clean, so orderly and even the smallest space was put to some useful purpose, only the mountains were untamed, we liked a bit of picturesque chaos rather than such unimaginative goodness!

When we returned to Cedar Cottage we found the children in good form and Christel as cheerful as ever. Fi was a little distant for the first few days, as if punishing us for leaving her.

Martin was fairly spoilt because he could wrap Christel round his little finger and get his own way. But with one or two adjustments we were soon back into the rhythm of family life with Cordelia into her second year at the village school and Tom Simon just beginning.

It was, I think, in the spring term that someone at Guildford suggested to Tom that we visit the Balearic Islands and said he knew of a village in Mallorca where we could rent a house. And that was how we arrived in Fornalutx for the first time, in the summer of 1956. This time we took Martin and left Fiona with friends who stayed at Cedar Cottage, Christel had by now left us and gone back to Germany. This, as you know, Jason, was where our dream came true. We bought what was then a rambling, dark barn of a building at a price we could afford and which we managed to pay for out of our war gratuities. It is now my only home and I hope I never have to leave it before I die. But that summer, so far away now, it was an exciting beginning.

We arrived in Fornalutx in the middle of a torrential electric storm. We parked in the *plaza* and out of the house which is now the *tapas* bar, rushed a *señora* with a huge black umbrella and shepherded us into her house where we waited for the rain to stop. When the skies cleared we were escorted up the steps by several people who carried our luggage, to the house we had rented from Lady Shepheard, an early resident of Fornalutx in the twenties. The house was nearly at the top of the village, *Son Figuera*, next to *Son Dichosa* which nowadays belongs to Bryony and Peter Cave, but in those days it was where Lady Shepheard stayed when she visited, with increasing rarity due to her age and impending blindness. When I went into the children's room there was still residual dripping from the storm and that was the start of my lifelong experience of leaking roofs in Mallorca.

Fornalutx and the valley of Sòller cast an immediate spell of enchantment over both Tom and myself and when we drove into the square on arrival, I had this uncanny sensation of coming home. We soon met the other three foreigners, Leonard Harrop, an Australian professor of Spanish who taught at the McGill University in Canada, John Polimeni or Giovanni (as it now says on his tomb) who was more Sicilian than British – he was a characteristic figure, limping through the village, waving his stick at some naughty child. What I remember most about him was his melodious tenor voice and his wicked jokes. Then there was a Mrs Dixon Clegg (Polly) who lived up the dirt road leading to the mountains. After World War I she and her husband spent the winters in Mallorca owing to her husband's poor health. By the time we knew her she was a widow and came in the summer. Of the three we saw most of Leonard Harrop who was very helpful to us in our lack of Spanish and in general information. He and Polimeni had bought a number of houses and ruins and it seemed their hobby to restore and equip them. The economic factor became more obvious as the years went by. We never looked at another house because no other house was presented to us and we were not into ruins. This house was solid, big enough for innovations, it was in this wonderful village and we could afford to buy it. That was all we needed.

Once we had decided to buy it Leonard introduced us to Don Tomàs Morell, a Sòller lawyer who arranged the sale and subsequently guided us in our renovation plans and oversaw the work in our absence. He and Tom became firm friends and the family have remained our friends to this day. Tom took photos of the two little children when we were invited to a Sunday lunch at their *finca* in the country between Fornalutx and Sòller. Early communication was in French with a little English and as time progressed smatterings of Spanish on our part. Don Tomàs was unfailingly helpful, courteous and kind. During Tom's final days and after his death, his practical help and support, and his friendship undoubtedly lightened my burden. Tomàs died the day before my brother Francis in August 1996 so that I felt bereft at one stroke of the two people to whom I could turn for advice on many things. His wife,

Barbara died just after Christmas 2005 and I miss meeting her on the streets of Sòller and exchanging family and local news.

After we bought the house that summer and when we returned to the UK, there were not a few people who thought we were quite mad and had been most unwise to buy a property on a Mediterranean island. But we knew better!

If things were going well for us at one level, at another they were working against us. It was not now possible to ignore entirely Tom's nephritis. About every two or three months he had devastating headaches, sometimes accompanied by vomiting. But after about half a day in bed, the attack passed and he was soon back to normal.

We spent another summer in Fornalutx getting our house gradually more habitable. The following autumn Tom had quite a bad dose of flu and the doctor kept him in bed longer that he would have done ordinarily. Pausing in the kitchen on his way out after one of his visits (doctors visited patents in those days) he said to me abruptly – "you do realise he's not going to last much longer?" I thought I had misheard him and asked him what he meant. His reply was – "I mean he's not going to live very long." I reminded him what the hospital had said, his late sixties and he was not yet fifty. Our doctor shrugged his shoulders – "I think they are being very, very optimistic." And with this parting shot, he left. I remember I had been constipated for the past couple of days and how this bombshell blasted my bowels as no laxative could have done. When I felt calmer I went up to our bedroom. Tom was sitting up in bed correcting an article for which the deadline was drawing near. He looked up, "Hullo, darling, the old quack says I can get up tomorrow and about time too, I need to get back to work. You know I think he's a bit overcautious." I didn't say anything but Tom didn't look or sound like a man who was going to die that soon.

But our real moment of truth arrived without warning. We woke up one miserable February morning and Tom asked me why I had removed all the jars and bottles from the shelf above the basin in our room. I said I hadn't, he replied, "I can't see them." I drew back the curtains on the window opposite to our bed and looked out on the hazy, miserably damp morning, the trees loomed black through the mist. "Can you see the trees?" I asked. "No, it's all grey fuzz." Our doctor arrived shortly after breakfast when the children had been taken off to school by a neighbour. He took one look at Tom and said he must go straight away to hospital. He made some phone calls from the house and told me the ambulance would come in about an hour. Later, as we sped along the Surrey lanes towards Roehampton Hospital an icy hand clutched at my heart. Tom was lying with his eyes closed and he was an unhealthy yellow colour.

It was February 1959. Towards the end of the previous year Tom had decided he would give up Guildford at the end of the following summer term and he had already sent in his letter of resignation. We had made up our minds to move the entire family to Fornalutx and to let Cedar Cottage. We hoped that the warmer climate and a more relaxed way of life would be a positive influence on Tom's illness. With a basic income from the Cedar Cottage rent, Tom was sure that we could manage with the additional income from his freelance work. Already various steps had been taken towards initiating the move.

Tom was three months in hospital and for one month he was on the danger list. My mother came to help me with the children and I drove up most days to Roehampton Hospital (which in those days was still an RAF hospital). I kept on with our arrangements to move to Fornalutx and I think people thought I was mad, but I am convinced it was one of the factors which contributed to Tom's recovery. After he was out of danger and his sight returned he kept on questioning me eagerly about what was happening. For a short few months Fate was kind to us and in June we drove in a leisurely manner out to Fornalutx in our brand new Ford van – a present from my mother.

Well, Jason, what a long letter! I hope it didn't bore you — life all those decades ago. I hope your move went well and you like the house.

Much love,
your loving grandma
Veronica

Dearest Thomas

Well, what a surprise, you're off to Australia, just like your grandad! Only Tom went when he was seventeen on an immigrant's passage, partly paid for by the Australian government for those wishing to settle in Australia. He had never been away from home in his life and he cried himself to sleep that first night at sea. He spent five years there, working long hours for small wages on big sheep stations in N.S. Wales. It was during the Depression in the late 1920s and nothing seemed to offer much of a future. He loved the open air life and he learned to ride and manage horses (he was always rather scornful of the English mode of riding which he regarded as prissy). He told me he had a harrow with eight horses to manage and he likened it to directing a ballet. When he set sail I was seven years old and had started at Miss Marwick's exclusive school, St. Monica's in Edinburgh. How different your visit will be and what a different country Australia now is. What your grandfather missed so much were kindred souls interested in books and music and art with whom he could exchange ideas. The general lack of stimulation he found depressing – all the farmers could talk about was the weather, the crops and the deteriorating situation.

It was 1942 when I set sail from Britain. Before the war 'across the Channel' was a big adventure. To be going to the Middle East seemed like the ends of the earth. At the time of my posting to Cairo I was still working at the Air Ministry in London only we had moved from our grand building in King Charles Street to a warren of underground offices built beneath the Horseferry Road, not far from Victoria Street. Rosemary and I, after our bomb episode, had moved out to Putney into a very nice flat with a lovely garden which we shared with the

121

owner, the photographer, Lotte Meitner Graf. It meant we had a long journey into work but it was worth it. Working all day by artificial light in an airless atmosphere was not very pleasant and when we emerged into the street at lunchtime the light made us blink.

By now the war had moved to North Africa and there were listening posts in the desert outside Cairo and Alexandria with a headquarters in Heliopolis, the big garden suburb of Cairo. More wireless intelligence personnel were needed and my boss in Horseferry Road asked me if I would like to volunteer. (Women volunteered for overseas service, they weren't sent willy nilly like the men.) It didn't take me five minutes to make up my mind. Anything to get out of Horseferry Road and what exotic images the name Cairo conjured up! I rang my mother that evening from the flat. "How long will you be away?" she asked. "Two to four years, but the war won't last that long," I tried to re-assure her. Rosemary was madly jealous and I promised to work on the powers-that-be the moment I got there so they would ask for her.

Once my posting was confirmed there came a round of jabs and getting various items of tropical kit assembled. Then a week's embarkation leave. Rosemary took some leave owing to her and together we travelled north to Edinburgh. We had been together for over two years and so the parting was quite a wrench.

My week's leave flew by, I saw a number of my friends and some of my relatives. Francis was home from the T.B. sanatorium in Aberdeen but not of course fit for military service, so he was back working at the office. Bud was still with the Atholls (the Duke was to die in March) and she came through to Edinburgh a couple of times to see me. We all went to the pantomime at the Kings Theatre, even my Dad! Rosemary went back to London the day before I left. Then, on a particularly cold, grey January morning, I found myself being waved goodbye in the Caledonian Station by my parents and Francis as the Glasgow train steamed away from the platform.

As they disappeared from view my heart thudded into my well polished shoes and I was invaded by momentary panic. But by the time we reached Gourock I was all agog and excited again.

What seemed to me to be complete chaos reigned on the docks at Gourock with officers and NCOs darting about with clipboards in their hands, checking up on people. It transpired that there were to be eight women travelling and soon they had us all herded together in one spot. There were three nursing sisters, three WAAF including myself and two civilians. Out in the middle of the misty Clyde I could discern an indistinct line of boats – our convoy. Fairly soon we were in a small motor boat chugging across the water to the line of ships and we tied up alongside what looked to be a big, big ship. The lower decks were lined with soldiers leaning over the rails and as we disembarked from the motor boat and clambered up the companionway we were followed by a chorus of wolf whistles.

The *Louis Pasteur* had been a French luxury liner plying between Bordeaux and various South American ports and not all traces of luxury had disappeared in its conversion to a British troopship. Gold leaf was prominent in the dining room and the lounges. Our berths were in what had been a large first class cabin but the beds and fittings had been removed and two sets of three tiered bunks installed, but we benefited from the en suite bathroom. The ship had just returned from Canada whence it had transported Canadian wounded and it had re-victualled there with food the quality of which we had not seen in a long time. Huge bowls of fruit stood on the sideboards in the dining room – oranges and bananas which had vanished from our shops and other more exotic fruits such as mangoes, melons and grapes. Not to mention the roast chickens, legs of lamb and sides of roast beef and as many eggs as we wanted.

We weighed anchor in the late afternoon around teatime and moved down the misty Clyde. Once out in the open sea, the convoy re-arranged itself, a bit like musical chairs and our naval escort fussing up and down like an overanxious governess. Finally we were all in order and got going properly as darkness was falling. The lighting was fairly dim on board and of course all the portholes and windows were blacked out. When I finally got to my bunk that night (I had managed to procure the top bunk and we WAAF slept on one set of bunks, the nursing sisters on the other) and curled myself up to sleep, I was acutely conscious that the sea beneath us could hold very unpleasant surprises, infested as it was by German submarines. But I managed to banish such thoughts and was soon asleep.

We were wakened the next morning by a steward bearing a tray with six mugs of steaming tea – a very unexpected service and I suppose laid on for senior officers and the women. All the kitchen staff and stewards were original members of the *Louis Pasteur's* crew in its cruise days. Our ship was transporting in the main Army personnel with a much smaller contingent of the RAF. I was somewhat dismayed that first morning when a message was brought from the Wing Commander that the senior WAAF was to report to his cabin, to find that I was the senior WAAF (marginally). The other two were both older than me and much more worldly wise. Binkie was divorced and quite hard-bitten but I liked her, Brenda was the epitome of the sexy blonde, but not dumb. I'm sure it was she who elicited all those wolf whistles as we came on board! So, there was nothing for it but to set off in search of the Wingco's cabin. I found him to be a big, good looking, middle-aged man with a roving eye and I have my suspicions that it fixed quite successfully on Brenda for the voyage's duration. He seemed acutely aware that we (the RAF) were dominated by a large Army majority and determined that we should not be overlooked or 'done down' where perks and privileges were concerned. "So," he concluded, "if you have any problems come straight to me. Remember I am your commanding officer and *no one else.* " "Yes, sir," I replied meekly, saluted and withdrew.

Two days at sea and we ran into some very rough Atlantic weather. The *Louis Pasteur* was a terrible roller and it was hard to keep one's balance. My cabin companions were soon laid low and groaning in their bunks. I am fortunate in never having suffered from sea sickness or loss of appetite in rough seas. So I slithered down from my top bunk and lurched my way to the dining room for breakfast. A faint cheer rose from the decimated ranks of the (mostly Army) officers as I made my way to the empty women's table ready to tuck into a plate of bacon and eggs. But if the officers were throwing up in their cabins what must conditions have been like on the lower decks where the unfortunate Other Ranks were packed like sardines. The lower decks were out of bounds to us women, but a young Lieutenant who went down daily to see how his men were faring, told me that conditions were really disgusting, Some chaps hadn't even got bunks and had to sleep on tables. Fortunately the rough weather didn't last long and soon everyone was up and about again with recovered appetites. As we sailed south it gradually became warmer and as we moved out of U-boat waters and enemy aircraft reach, the blackout became less stringent. In fact we managed to get permission to pull back the curtain and open the door on to the little deck outside our cabin, which gave us a bit of air at night.

It was not particularly enjoyable being such a tiny minority, some chap was always trying to chat one up or offer one a drink and unless you retired to the cabin it was difficult to get any time to yourself. There wasn't a lot to do apart from periodic boat drills. We had no official duties at all, at least the male officers had their chaps to look after. So it was mainly a round of meals and drinking. Booze was crazily cheap and the saloon lounge bar was open an hour before lunch and closed at 2 p.m. and then two hours before dinner and thereafter into the wee small hours. I never bought myself a single drink on that boat and apart from shorts in the lounge, our steward frequently brought a bottle of wine to our table, presented by some well wisher who would wave to us across the dining room. Then there were the senior officers' drinks parties in their more ample cabins and an invitation to any of these was not so much an invitation as a command. Not so long after this voyage all troopships were made dry. There had been several happenings at sea which might have turned out less disastrously had the ship's company been sober.

When Rosemary and I crossed from Egypt to Italy in 1944 the ship's bar sold soft drinks only. The nursing sisters kept themselves very much to themselves and regarded us WAAF with a faintly disapproving air. They always retired to the cabin immediately after dinner and rarely appeared in the saloon lounge – perhaps wisely. One of them was much younger than the other two and I think she would gladly have escaped their vigilance. They were of course under Army command; the O.C. Troops was a rather doddering looking oldish Colonel who might well have come out of a book on Army caricatures, but he had a very efficient Adjutant. The Captain commanding the vessel was a crusty old Aberdonian who liked his booze. He sent for me at the start of the voyage to tell me – "I want no pregnant women aboard my ship." I really did not know what he was trying to say but presumed it was his roundabout way of saying – no fornication. So I mumbled – "I understand, sir." Though what he thought I could do about it, I didn't know! The civilians kept themselves pretty much to themselves though not as much as the nursing sisters. I had no idea where their cabin was. As civilians they had greater freedom of decision than we had, if they chose not to turn up at a party no comment was made. So the time passed, I wrote home, tried to read, tried to keep as sober as possible and we had endless rehearsals for a ship's concert which we gave on three evenings before reaching Freetown. In the end it was a great success and went down well especially with the chaps from the lower decks who had been invited to be part of the audience, drawn by lots. Goodness knows we had little enough to occupy ourselves with, they were ten times worse off.

Finally we sailed into Freetown bay and dropped anchor. This was where I got off, the rest of my journey was to be by air, they wanted me sooner rather than later in Cairo. But no instructions or information was filtered through to me. When I went to the Wing Commander to ask him what was happening he said he had no instructions as yet – "Just you stay put," he said. So I joined the others at the rails watching small black boys diving for coins the men threw into the water.

All around us was a great deal of boat activity, members of the indigenous population trying to sell fruit and trinkets. The favourite headgear seemed to be the top hat and every second word began with F. "What does it mean?" I asked Brenda. She gave me a funny look – "You don't know? No. I'll tell you later." By 'later' I had fathomed it out for myself! (Here we could fast forward a couple of decades to when your aunt Cordelia, aged 12 asked me the very same question when we were making beds in Fornalutx. Pusillanimously I gave exactly the same answer substituting the word 'older' for 'later'. She found someone of her own peer group to enlighten her.)

It was excruciatingly hot in Freetown bay, hot and humid. We had discarded our 'blues' and were dressed in khaki cotton skirts and short-sleeved shirts but it wasn't much help and the air hummed with flies and other insects. Freetown, the capital of Sierra Leone, was established in 1792 as a home for freed slaves who had fought on the British side in the American War of Independence. In 1808 the British annexed the country to make it into a Crown Colony which it remained until independence in 1961.

That evening we received, via the Wing Commander, a surprise invitation to dinner on shore. Apparently there was a small RAF signals unit up the hill above Freetown and they had got wind of the fact that there were three WAAF officers on board the troopship that was anchored in the bay below them. Their O.C. had sent a signal to ours asking for permission to invite us to supper at their mess. Did we want to go? he asked. Of course we wanted to go, anything to get off the ship for a few hours. So that evening we were ferried ashore in a small tender which came to pick us up. At the jetty we were met by the Adjutant in a jeep and driven up a steep, bendy road to a collection of military huts at the top. We were ushered into the mess and immediately pressed to drinks. The C.O. who was a Squadron Leader introduced himself and still seemed reasonably sober. I remember him as having the most deeply brown eyes so that they appeared almost black. His name was Hazlitt and I wondered whether he had any connection with the 18th century essayist of that name. But when I asked him later he looked at me blankly.

Eventually we sat down, there were about ten of us altogether, round a table covered with a really filthy tablecloth. We were then served a totally tasteless, unidentifiable stew by a very sullen looking native servant whose white apron was about as dirty as the tablecloth. The men washed this down with quantities of beer and we girls were given some very peculiar white wine. A bowl of fruit was put on the table for dessert. I peeled mine with great care and then someone said – "it's all washed, you know." Yes, I thought, but in what sort of water? Finally we were served coffee, which was the best part of the meal, and the liqueurs were brought out. The rest of the evening was spent trying to drink as little as possible and fending off vague amorous advances. By now even Squadron Leader Hazlitt's dark eyes had a glazed look.

By 11.30 I was beginning to get fidgety about catching the tender to take us back to the ship. I knew the last run left at midnight and that I would be in deep trouble if we missed it. "Don't worry, don't worry, we'll get you there in time. Why don't we take the lorry and all go and see them off," one bright spark suggested. His suggestion was taken up with enthusiasm and so we had to clamber into the back of the lorry and were then driven at breakneck speed down this terrible twisting road by one of the officers who was certainly in no state to be behind a driving wheel. I really was terrified and I thought I've survived the London Blitz just to crash to my death in a lorry full of inebriated RAF officers. But miraculously we arrived on the jetty to a screech of brakes, unharmed. The tender was already hooting its signal of imminent departure so there was not much time for farewells. We teetered across the gang plank and the tender cast off to the shouts of farewell and whoops of our hosts, the sound of which pursued us across the water. Was I glad to return 'home' and although we tried to be as quiet as possible in the cabin inevitably we made noise which drew forth a caustic comment from the senior nursing sister. It's easy to be judgmental, but these poor devils had been stuck on that barren cliff top for months, probably doing a boring job, far from their homes and loved ones. It's easy to forget this aspect of war, at least in this particular war, the swathes of boredom that often have to be endured and people have to have profound inner resources to cope with it, all too often drink is the easiest means of escape.

The next morning the Wing Commander sent for me. "I've had a signal from Cairo, you are to proceed by air when an aircraft is available. In the meantime you will have to go to the depot ship to wait for it. We are leaving tomorrow so you better get your kit together and the tender will pick you up around midday."

So finally I had my marching orders. It didn't take me very long to get my things together, my heavy stuff was in the hold and I wouldn't see that until the ship had arrived in Suez, all I really had at the moment was hand luggage. I wasn't sorry to be leaving the ship which had all those weeks ahead before it reached Suez, although I would liked to have seen Cape Town. Soon I was in the tender and waving goodbye to my friends and everyone else hanging over the rails. "See you in Cairo," we shouted to one another as the tender took me away from the ship.

It didn't take long to reach the depot ship which was really quite a small boat. In peacetime it had belonged to a British coastal company and had plied up and down the Ivory Coast carrying goods and supplies. Now it acted as a sort of transit camp or hotel, however you liked to view it. I was shown to my cabin by a friendly Sierra Leonese steward and how I appreciated a cabin to myself, small though it was. I was apparently the only transient at the moment and at lunch I met the Flight Lieutenant who ran the administration and two gruff, bearded seamen who told me they belonged to the coastal company that owned the boat and were there for the duration to look after the engine and generally keep the boat seaworthy, although at the moment it did not go to sea. Despite their gruff manner they were friendly in a paternal way towards me and wondered what a girl like me was doing skittering about the world! I think they must have been of retirement age. The Flight Lieutenant, or the Adjutant as he was usually called was not a happy man. He told me that the job was deadly boring and he had been doing it for nearly a year. He had applied to London for a transfer but nobody had replied to his request. The consequences of his boredom were usually visible by lunchtime, though his outward behaviour was impeccable. There was no bar on board but alcohol was obviously obtainable and I was very glad when the steward offered me a beer with my lunch, I didn't want withdrawal symptoms! It was a luxury to go to my cabin after the meal and lie on my bunk and read as I hadn't done since leaving home.

The next morning I watched, from the stern of the depot ship, the departure of the *Louis Pasteur* and its now much smaller convoy. As it moved slowly out of the bay I mentally wished them well in their six weeks or so voyage round the Cape and up through the Red Sea to Suez, I felt as if I had escaped from a crazy institution. I remained for three days on the depot ship during which time I mainly read and wrote letters. We had two Poles for one night and they lightened the atmosphere considerably. Then on the afternoon of my third day the Adjutant told me there was an aircraft taking off the following morning early which I was to go on.

The steward wakened me at 4.30 a.m. with a mug of tea and a piece of buttered toast. Just after five I was in the tender and moving towards the shore in complete darkness. On the jetty was a largish minibus type vehicle in which there were a number of people, some military, some civilian. I climbed in and sat by a window. A few other people followed me at intervals. Nobody spoke and then eventually a driver arrived and closed the doors. We drove out of Freetown on a bumpy dirt road and gradually into the burgeoning dawn.

I had never flown in my life and was a bit nervous but at the same time excited. After about half an hour we arrived at a large piece of scrub land, you couldn't really call it a field, where there were a few military huts, a number of G.I.s and a DC4 plane. We transferred from the bus into the aircraft and after a short wait the pilot arrived. "Hi, folks. We're for off. First stop Monrovia," was how he greeted us. Then someone swung the propeller, the engine was started and the plane taxied to the far end of the 'field'.

My first take-off was a very bumpy one but I was so occupied looking at the wonderful dawn light through my window that I barely noticed. We flew to Liberia and came down at Monrovia. There seemed to be a great deal of activity here with important looking black gentlemen bustling about in tails and top hats. Most of the civilian passengers left us here. The rest of us got off and went to the cafeteria for some refreshment, then the pilot rounded us up and we were off again.

My first night's stop was at Accra and I was lodged in a Nurses' Home. I had a whitewashed cell-like room with a narrow iron bed and a basin with a ewer of cold water in the corner. I wondered nervously if there were any snakes and looked under the bed. At supper that night I was placed next to Matron and I felt very junior and rather as if I were back at boarding school. The conversation was a bit sticky but I didn't feel that my experiences over the past few weeks were exactly suitable for this particular supper table. After supper a very young Pilot Officer turned up to take me out and show me Accra. "Now mind you don't bring her back late," he was told by Matron. I remember nothing of that evening nor does any aspect of Accra present itself but he did land me back at the Home by 9.30.

I think the next day was quite a late start and we flew to Lagos without a stop. I overnighted there in quite a big RAF station and my most pungent memory is of after supper in the mess when we were quietly sipping our coffee and smoking our cigarettes, an officer rushed in, pulled out his revolver and shot the electric light bulbs. We were plunged in darkness but soon someone produced a strong torch and they disarmed their comrade and hustled him outside where I believe they hosed him down. He was a French Canadian Flight Lieutenant and the French Canadians had a reputation for being macho and given to showing off.

The plane I travelled on the following day had been stripped down to carry freight, so there were no seats. It was a question of sitting on the floor or perching on one of the wooden cases that were being carried. I chose the floor because I could stretch my legs out. I can't remember how many other passengers there were but I think three or four. After we had been in the air for some time, the pilot turned round and said to me – "Say, mam, would you like to fly this kite?"

Would I like to fly? You bet I would. So I got into the co-pilot's seat (we had no co-pilot) and took over the joystick. It was so easy and so logical, up to ascend, down to descend, right to turn right and left to turn left. I was in my element. "Go down," the pilot said, "right down quite low and we'll see the lions on the rocks beneath us." Sure enough, there was a group of lions lying basking in the sunshine. I made up my mind to have flying lessons when I got to Cairo but like so many dreams it never transpired, there wasn't the time. Now flying is my least favourite mode of transport.

We landed at Kano for lunch. I was taken to the RAF mess and as we ate lunch I kept looking nervously over my shoulder at the very sizable lion cub which padded round and round the table. "Don't be nervous," the officer sitting next to me said, "he's very tame and we all love him, he's our mascot." Nevertheless I was relieved when lunch was over and someone suggested they take me and show me the market before I had to leave. I was glad to get out into the blinding sunshine.

We walked round the stalls which sold leather goods and materials, there wasn't time to go to the food market which would have been more interesting. I loved the vivid colouring of the Nigerians' dress. Back in the same plane again we flew north to Maiduguri. I had to hang around the American PX for a while until transport could be found to take me to the RAF unit which was outside Maiduguri. At last a G.I. waved to me from the door and I was taken in a Dodge van (I hadn't seen one of them since my Dalmeny days) about ten minutes into the country.

I was set down outside an attractive, countrified house with a great sweep of gravel in front of it. It was very quiet and there seemed to be absolutely nobody about and then down the steps came a native servant in a spotless white gown. He smiled and raised his arms in a gesture of uncertainty – "No back yet, duck shooting, I show you room." I followed him into the house and up the stairs into a room that obviously belonged to someone but who had thoughtfully cleared the bedside table and dropped a couple of hangers on the bed. "I bring tea," said my host and disappeared. I looked around me, there were books and records on the chairs and on the window sill a series of carved figures, both human and animal. There were two figures about ten inches high, a man and a woman facing one another in full sexual arousal. Hmph, I thought to myself, you won't find souvenirs like that in the shops in Princes Street. There was a tap on my door – tea had arrived and in a teapot too, admittedly rather battered. After I had drunk my tea, I took my skirt off and lay down on the bed. I was very tired. I came to, to the sound of tyres on the gravel below and then voices and feet coming into the house. I roused myself and got up, splashed some cold water on my face and went out on the landing to meet my real hosts.

My stop-over in Maiduguri has remained extraordinarily vivid in my memory even after all these years. It's not so much a memory of people and happenings as the memory of the atmosphere there which has stayed with me. Perhaps because it was the absolute antithesis of that other unit in Freetown. It was also a small unit (I don't know what they did, one didn't ask people in wartime what they did unless they were part of one's own outfit) and admittedly they lived in much more attractive surroundings. The C.O. was of quite junior rank, I can't remember, but not more than a Flight Lieutenant and there were about five other officers. I don't know where the O.R.s were housed or how many there were.

That evening we had an extremely good dinner, beautifully served by the servant who had first admitted me. With it we drank wine, but in sips rather than in gulps. Overhead a punkah wafted to and fro, worked by a small boy seated on a cushion and pulling on a rope. He seemed a bit of a joker and every now and again threw remarks at his father who was waiting on us, his father laughed and so did the rest of us. After dinner we took chairs out on the gravel in front of the house and sat in a semi-circle to have our coffee under a dark, velvety sky studded with so many brilliant stars. It was quite magical. It was warm and miraculously insect free and strange distant calls and hoots came floating through the night air towards us. I had a very early start the following day and the C.O. said to me that they didn't want to keep me up late and to go to bed whenever I wanted. So regretfully I left their friendly company and after thanking the chap who had given up his room for me and was doubling up for the night with someone else, I went up to bed.

The next morning I was wakened at 4.30 with a cup of tea and a small slice of buttered toast and at 5 a.m. sharp I heard tyres on the gravel below. I went downstairs and the servant opened the door and I slipped out. I was driven to the PX where I had a hearty American breakfast, including waffles!

I was the only passenger on the plane that morning when we took off to fly to Khartoum, my last stop before Cairo, but there was a lot of freight and it was difficult to find a corner to sit down comfortably. We landed briefly at Fort Lamy in Chad to pick up a Free French colonel who came on board looking very dapper in a freshly pressed uniform. He gave me a rather supercilious look and after a curt *bon jour* never addressed another word to me. By now I was feeling and looking decidedly travel stained and scruffy. The colonel perched himself on a packing case and took some important looking papers out of his briefcase and perused them all the way to Khartoum.

It was in Khartoum that I learned my first Arabic word. I was housed in quite a big RAF station and that evening the Adjutant and a couple of other officers took me out to dinner in a restaurant in the town. As we looked at the menu the Adjutant looked up and said − "Shall we drink *moya*?" I thought I was going to be introduced to some new exotic drink and was somewhat disappointed when the waiter poured ice cold water into my glass! But what was really extraordinary was that towards the end of the evening we were treated to a very good cabaret show by Europeans and I was told that they were Austrian and therefore enemy aliens. They were locked up during the day and allowed out at night to give their performance. I wondered how long they would have to remain prisoners by day and performers by night. I supposed for the duration but I never heard what was their eventual fate.

I have no memory of the flight to Cairo except vaguely, as we descended coming in over the Pyramids. I was met by a WAAF officer whom I had known in the UK, in fact she was the very one who had been present at the Air Ministry at my initial interview. How long ago all that seemed now. She took me to an hotel in the centre of Cairo, somewhere at the back of Shepheards Hotel and told me I was to get a good night's rest and she would pick me up the following morning and take me out to Heliopolis where I would be working. After she left I went out on to the small balcony of my room and looked about me. Immediately in front of me was a sign, on a smaller building than a hotel, which read 'Maternity Home'. It made me think of the boozy old Captain of the *Louis Pasteur*. I hadn't given any of them a moment's thought during my journey but now I wondered how they were all getting on. Most of the hoardings which I could see were in Arabic and so didn't tell me much. The sounds rising from the street were distinctly strange to my unaccustomed ear. Then I heard a sound which rose above all the others and I suddenly realised that it must the *muezzin* from a nearby mosque calling the faithful to prayer. Indeed I was a long way from Horseferry Road. This was to be my home for the next two years.

Anyway, Thomas, that is the story of my journey to the Middle East and I hear, on speaking to your Mum on the phone last night, that you are *not* now going to Australia. Not sufficient money and too many debts. Never mind, just get working and pay them off and I'm sure you will get to Australia one of these days if you really want to.

Lots of love and work hard,

your loving g'ma Veronica

Dearest Damian

I wonder how you are getting on with job hunting and whether you have had your interview yet with the primary school? It is a long, tedious business trying to find something that one actually *likes* doing and so many people never do.

When we finally returned to Cedar Cottage from Fornalutx in March 1962, that's to say Martin, Fiona and myself (your mother, Cordelia and Tom Simon, as he was still called, having gone back to boarding school in September 1961), I knew that eventually I would have to find a job, but where or what I had no idea. But owing to the deplorable condition of our poor house by the uncaring tenants who had lived there, I postponed the decision for several months, my immediate priority being to return the house and the grounds to a reasonable state. So after the Easter holidays I set to, papering and painting, digging and weeding nearly every day of the week and sometimes at night time as well. Most of the renovation I did myself and only paid for other people to do what was beyond my competence. By the summer it was looking distinctly freshened up and clean, more of a home, in fact. However I was beginning to wonder whether I really wanted to stay on there and from the point of view of getting a job it didn't seem as if there would be a great deal of choice. I wasn't sure that I could cope with living on my own with the children in this Surrey woodland, rodding the pipes to the septic tank when they got blocked, unfreezing the water pipes in a severe winter. Besides which I felt the time had come for change. What had been for Tom and myself an idyllic situation to bring up our young family no longer seemed to apply to me on my own with children approaching adolescence.

So… where was I to move to? In my young days London had always been my Mecca and Tom and I had lived in immediate post-war London for nearly a year. So London it was – and what a contrast to Newdigate!

On reflection and in today's climate of opinion, I could be accused of not consulting the children, which I didn't. I was brought up to believe that it was adults who made the decisions and that children should not be burdened with unnecessary responsibilities. I would even risk sticking my head above the parapet by saying that today I do think children are given too many choices. I could be wrong, but be that as it may, mine were not consulted. If they had been I expect we would have remained where we were.

I eventually bought a top floor flat in Eccleston Square, at the back of Victoria Station, the square where Rosemary and I had experienced our bombing out. I don't quite know what drew me back there but I had lived in Pimlico for most of the Blitz and maybe I wanted to experience it in peacetime. I certainly knew that I wanted to live relatively centrally and not out in the suburbs. The flat was purchased shortly after my mother's death in 1964. She had been coming to visit me that summer in Fornalutx and suffered a stroke the night before her flight. Luckily Bud was with her at the time. She was in a nursing home for three months unable to speak or move. Both Bud and I were at her bedside when she died. She was 77. And so I lost my beloved mother five years after Tom.

I was lucky enough to sell Cedar Cottage to friends, Alison and Martin Hughes. Alison had been a student of Tom's at Guildford and they had two small boys. This meant that we did not entirely lose touch with Cedar Cottage and we used to visit quite frequently. One thing which upset the children (and me) was that Alison and Martin dismantled the tree house almost immediately on moving in, the house that Tom had so enjoyed building with occasional help from our neighbour, Denis Upton, and which had been a source of such delight for the children to play in and to learn to climb up and to swing down on the tyre safely and without fear. But maybe they were more safety conscious parents than we were!

Magdalena came from Fornalutx to help me move. She had a Mallorquin friend who was married to an Englishman who lived in Cornwall whom she visited. Then before I moved to London, during the summer holidays, we went on a joint pony trekking holiday with the Irvines at Blair Atholl. The two youngest members of each family, Jo and Fi, were regarded as too young for such a holiday and so stayed behind in the Rectory at Callender with Tur and Magdalena. Thus Magdalena had quite a varied view of the UK.

The actual move to London took place once the elder children had gone back to school. Fiona stayed with her aunt and uncle in Callender for the autumn term and went to Jo's PNEU school. Once the move was completed, Magdalena went back home to Mallorca and I was left to contemplate the prospect of getting work. It had to be compatible with Fi's school hours. When she returned from Scotland she went to a PNEU school in London and I delivered and fetched her in the car. So work-wise I would have to start late and finish early. This didn't leave me a great deal of choice.

My first job turned out to be in market research. I hated it. I didn't have to accost people in the street but was sent each month a list of names and addresses in my area together with a sheaf of interview forms to be filled in (by me). So I went round ringing doorbells and sometimes there was no reply and sometimes the door was shut in my face which was what I secretly hoped for! But mostly people were very polite and long suffering and invited me in. Several of the questions I had to ask I found intrusive and some I had to ask were so worded as to obtain information which had little to do with the product in question. I forget what it was now, something boring like a heating apparatus, I think. Then at the end of each month I had to send in my forms, tick the addresses visited and whether I had obtained entry or not and finally a check list of the hours worked. The pay was pretty measly and after three or four months I packed it in.

My next job was with the WRVS. The Women's Voluntary Services had done stalwart work during the war, setting up and running canteens for the troops on railway stations and elsewhere and generally occupying themselves with welfare activities. After the war they were granted a Royal Charter. But I became a paid employee and worked in their property maintenance department at their headquarters near St. James Park tube station. The WRVS owned properties or had repairing leases on houses in many towns around Britain from where they operated. It was my job to deal with some of the requests for repairs and to contact builders, painters and decorators and, if the requests were given the OK by the top brass, to arrange for the work to be carried out. I seem to remember there were a lot of leaking roofs. The day-to-day work consisted of writing letters and making telephone calls. It wasn't very exciting but it was streets ahead of market research (so-called).

By this time Fiona had left her day school in London and was now at King Edwards school near Godalming as a full-time boarder. So this enabled me to work a full day. I have no memory of what I got paid but it was a formal contract and I got paid holidays. Your Mum was now a weekly boarder and came home at the weekends from her school in Worthing, which was nice. She was around sixteen and well able to manage her own affairs. But the great plus of the WRVS job was getting to know Fleur Bethlen. She too worked in the maintenance department and our desks were opposite to one another.

Fleur was Rumanian, a highly cultured and intelligent woman with a wonderful sense of humour and we quickly became friends and most days took our lunch hour together. We found the same things funny at work, particularly some of the voluntary ladies who were our bosses. Fleur had lived in dire circumstances during the war and after, both under the

140

fascists and the communists, inhabiting bombed-out buildings with two small children, very little to eat and fetching rationed water from a communal standpipe. She was a very good looking woman with beautiful bone structure in her face and wide-set Slavonic eyes. She was a great Anglophile and had been all her life. There was little she didn't know about English literature and she admired what she saw as British moderation in our politics. Her English was fluent with the faintest of accents. I suppose it was mainly a work friendship although I did meet her family latterly. Her husband, a Rumanian count, was the manager of a factory somewhere in north London, they had two grown-up daughters, the elder of which was a nurse but her Rumanian qualifications were not recognised in the UK.

Curiously enough Fleur lived quite near me in a mansion block in Buckingham Palace Road and they all lived together with her brother-in-law who was a designer of furniture and apparatus for the disabled and an elderly lady who was either her mother, or her husband's. It is one of my great regrets that I lost touch with her. When I left the WRVS we saw one another now and again and kept in touch during my first year as a social worker at Westminster. But without the daily work contact, and my full workload plus home happenings, it became increasingly difficult to keep contact. Something I now deeply regret. Eventually the mansion block of flats was pulled down and the Bethlen family moved, to Richmond.

I worked for the WRVS for about eighteen months but the work didn't satisfy me. I felt I wanted something more than just a 'job', I wanted something more professional, something for which I could be trained and at the end be qualified. One day I saw an advertisement in *New Society* for applicants to train as Probation Officers. I had always been interested in courts of law and remembered as a young girl going with my mother on one or two occasions to the Edinburgh Sheriff court to hear some interesting case. I knew a little bit about what Probation Officers did. Life experience was one of the qualities they were looking for. Well I'd had a bit of that hadn't I? I sent away for an application form. The whole process of applying took about nine months, several preliminary interviews, a day spent with a probation team, building up to a whole day final session. I had made it through to the last hurdle. I was pretty confident, thought I would make a good probation officer and had begun to visualise myself in this role. I should have scented danger when at my final interview, one of the interviewers asked: "Do you not think, Mrs Weedon, that your life experience has better equipped you to work with children, say in a Children's Department of some local authority?" No, I did not. I had just about finished rearing four children single-handed and I had enough of children and would much prefer to work with adults. Three weeks later there was an anonymous looking little brown envelope in the post. I opened it and drew out a flimsy slip of paper – *we regret you have not been selected for training as a Probation Officer*. My confidence bubble was severely pricked and I continued dealing with leaking roofs and painting contracts for the WRVS.

Some weeks later I was reading my *New Society* and came across an advert for mature students to train as Child Care Officers, so that's what the probation lot must have been on about, I thought, and sent for an application form. I examined what my defects must have been to cause my rejection for training as a probation officer and the most obvious was that I had not had any experience of social work in even a voluntary capacity. I set about remedying this and got accepted as a volunteer family adviser by the Blackfriars Settlement in Southwark and worked one evening a week and one whole Sunday a month. I was summonsed by the Child Care people for a day-long process of intelligence tests, essay writing and interviews. At the end of the day I was walking back to the Underground with one of the other candidates and she said to me, "You know there are three hundred applicants and only nineteen places." Well, I thought, you can forget about that, you're never going to get a place.

Around this time, friends of mine who had a cottage in a coastal village near Swansea spoke about wanting to find someone to house-sit for them. They only used it in the summer and it became very damp through lack of occupation. The desire to write hovered continuously on the periphery of my life but since Tom's death I had only written one article, published in the *Daily Telegraph*, on the home schoolroom. But I really wanted to write novels. There still remained in my psyche, the little girl who had answered her mother's teatime visitors with such scorn when they enquired what she wanted to be when she grew up – a writer of course.

I put Child Care Officering out of my mind, there would be no future for that. I began to visualise a different future. I could probably rent my flat for a reasonable sum which would help to put food on the table, the children would come to South Wales for the Christmas and Easter holidays and in the summer we would go to Fornalutx. I was not going to be asked to pay rent, just the bills. The prospect of at last taking the plunge and sitting down to write day after day was exciting and I looked forward to this change of direction. But it was not to be. I received a letter summoning me to a final interview and a week later I was offered a place on a two-year course of social work training. The pleasure of my acceptance was double-edged but no way could I do other than accept it. The children were not yet grown up, I had a responsibility to work and supply their needs and if I passed this course successfully, I would have a permanent full-time job. But it was with regret that I turned my back on what may well have been a hare-brained scheme.

I was the eldest on my course, forty-eight, the youngest was twenty-two and the rest were mainly in their thirties or early forties. I enjoyed it thoroughly, to be actually *expected* to read so many books was a luxury. Reading had become a rare activity for me during the past years, there never seemed time. I got very tired especially during the school holidays when I had to make arrangements for the children. My practical placements were arranged for term time so that didn't cause problems.

By now Cordelia was at Guildford Art School studying photography and Tom was working on a farm in Wiltshire which only left Martin and Fiona as still dependant. In the summer we all foregathered in Fornalutx and I wrote my essays in the summer heat. On the last summer when the course was over and I had obtained a job in the Children's Department of Westminster City Council and was due to start at the beginning of September, I had my famous fall. I had just dropped Cordelia off at the airport and returned to Deià to collect Fiona and Martin from a party at the Graves. I parked my car on a steep road against the wall of a house. When I returned to it later after dark, I misdirected myself and fell about six feet over the edge of one steep road onto the hard stony surface of the one below, fracturing my right wrist and breaking my left knee in the fall.

That put a real spanner in the works as I was about to drive back home with Martin and Fiona in a few days' time, instead of which I languished in appalling heat in a Palma clinic with my left leg and my right arm in plaster. Arrangements had to be made to get the two of them back for school and two French friends of Beryl and Robert drove them in my car to the Channel and put them and the car on the ferry. Tom met them on the other side and drove them to London where Cordelia was ensconced in Eccleston Square prior to going back to Guildford.

My neighbours Valerie and Robert Goulet brought me back to Fornalutx and a strong village man carried me up the steps to my house. My friend Fleur from WRVS days visited me with her elder daughter. They were a bit diffident about coming in view of my accident but I said if they could look after themselves it was no bother and it was cheering to have their company as I was very immobile. Also Fleur's daughter worked wonders on my mangled big toe. It had small particles of dusty grit and stone embedded in the soft pad and was speckled with dried blood. The clinic had mended my broken limbs but they had no interest in my poor toe. I sat with my foot in the bidet while with great care and gentleness she prised all the extraneous bits out of my flesh and cleaned it all up. I could not have reached it myself because of the plaster cast on my leg. I went back to London by air accompanied by Tomàs Graves who was going back to school at Bedales. At the flat we found Cordelia who had cooked a nice meal and made up my bed, so my homecoming was effortless.

However she had to leave the next day to return to Guildford and I had to get used to functioning left-handed and with a rigid leg. By now I had written to Westminster and informed them of what had happened. I presumed that they would postpone my starting date but apparently it was easier from an administrative point of view simply to put me on sick leave and so I started my career at Westminster on sick pay. The doctors in Palma had said that the plasters should remain on for about six weeks.

At the appropriate time I went to St. Georges Hospital at Hyde Park corner and had the casts removed. I was told to attend a 'leg clinic' for physiotherapy, they weren't interested in my wrist which had suffered a second time round fracture. I attended this clinic, at which there were about eight people, twice only. The physiotherapist, who was German, was an unsympathetic character who shouted at us, I thought she would make a good candidate for a concentration camp guard! I invented my own therapy, walking up and down the four flights of stairs in the house twice a day, bending my knee (and did it hurt) at every step.

Finally I was fit to take up my duties at Westminster towards the end of October, nearly two months late. I enjoyed the work of a Child Care Officer, I also enjoyed the pay (£1300 a year, the same as Tom had been paid at Guildford as a Senior Lecturer in the fifties and rather better than the £260 a year I had earned immediately post war in the forties). I was in a team with whom I got on well and my senior was an avuncular seeming chap, but on the ball, practical and supportive I can't say my view of some of the members of the higher echelons was so favourable, however I didn't have much to do with them and they were not on my back. It was a fairly formal atmosphere in which we worked in those days, everyone was Mr or Miss or Mrs, and women were not allowed to wear trousers, at least during my first year there.

It was at Westminster that I met my dear friend Lore Sproule, whom you all know, and I am happy that this friendship has survived into old age despite our different lifestyles and the fact that we live 2,000 miles apart. Owing to my age (I was fifty when I started work at Westminster in 1969) and life experience, I had a large number of adolescents on my case load, some of them delinquent and this meant I had a fair amount of court work which I always found interesting. What I most enjoyed about the job was the independence one had in organising each working day (or week).

I suppose ever since the war, when one was moved about like a pawn on a board and the course of your life was ordered by others with little or no say so on your own part, I have always felt enormous appreciation of the autonomy returned to the individual in peacetime. It's a long time ago now since the war, but I still have flashes of that appreciation when I wake up in the morning and know that I am my own commanding officer! Certainly a Child Care Officer's job was no nine to five routine and sometimes I would return home around 10 p.m. if I had been out of London visiting a child or an institution. I was not much concerned with the number of hours I worked but with doing the job well to my own satisfaction. I dare say things are very different nowadays and people wouldn't dream of working long hours without financial compensation for overtime. Neither would I if I had been working in a boring job, but my job wasn't boring.

Come 1972 and the Seebohm Report which caused a radical change in the structure of social work with the introduction of the generic social worker. Social work was now to be carried out in the round and no longer broken up among the different needs. Children's Departments and Child Care Officers were out, Social Work Departments and generic Social Workers were in. I can't say this pleased me personally – I had no desire to work with the elderly, the mentally handicapped, nor the physically handicapped – I wanted to stay with young people. To this end I joined the department's adoption agency where there was a vacancy. The adoption agency was run by Lore. It was quite different work which I had to learn, I enjoyed it and worked there for eighteen months. We were a small, cohesive team and Lore ran it with efficiency and humour. At the end of eighteen months I left Westminster in order to go and spend three months in Fornalutx.

I had bought a small unmodernised cottage in Wiltshire, near Devizes and to this I escaped as many weekends as I could. Bolt Cottage, named after its previous owner, George Bolt, an eccentric Wiltshire man, was indeed my bolt hole. Away from London, from work responsibilities and quite substantial personal worries, I would get out of the car on a Friday evening and draw a deep breath of the fresh country air and feel my problems evaporating. While it was in its primitive state, I had few visitors, but Uncle Hugh died and left me three thousand pounds and so I was able to modernise it. After that it became quite a popular rendezvous.

I was beginning to wonder vaguely whether, when I retired, I would want to stay in Wiltshire or move to Fornalutx. With this in mind, I went to Fornalutx for three months in the winter, a time of year when it is damp, often quite cold and with no one much about other than the villagers. (I am talking about thirty-odd years ago, Damian.) The house was still fairly primitive with only the wood fire to heat it and I wanted to live there during a period when I would not be seduced by the charms of spring and early summer. I made my choice, as you know, and I have never regretted it.

I had not necessarily intended to work again for Westminster but that was how it turned out when I came back.

I got a post as Homes' Advisor and it was senior to my previous post so I earned more money. It was very different sort of work, giving support to residential staff and acting as a trouble-shooter where necessary. I attended case reviews of children in the homes and was involved in the interviewing and appointment of residential staff. My colleague, the other Homes' Advisor, Joan Ramelson, was a lovely person and we saw eye to eye in most things. She is one of the few Westminster people I am still in touch with, if intermittently. As retirement drew nearer, I had the idea of working part-time for the last year or so, partly as a winding down process, but more particularly because I wanted to learn to be a potter. My first interest in pottery had been aroused at school, very briefly, and that had been that. But I had visions of making it an activity of my retirement.

Again for my last job I was employed by Westminster. I became a part-time fostering officer and was involved in finding foster parents and placing children. This was a drop in seniority and I was back to being a basic social worker. I worked three days a week and the other two I spent attending whole day pottery classes. Once again I worked in a team and my senior was someone who had been a child care officer in my original team, somebody whom I knew quite well. I think she was faintly embarrassed at being my senior. "Veronica," she said to me once, "I would have thought you would have wanted to be a senior yourself, or may be something even more." Ambition has been sorely lacking, I suppose, in my attitudes. I am not single-minded which could be seen as a defect. I have a sort of impressionistic attitude to life. The only area where I would have appreciated success and recognition would have been as a writer.

So I finished my short working life (my paid working life) as a part-time fostering officer. I was neither sorry nor glad to give up work, I had enjoyed my work but another period of life was coming up on the screen and I had plenty of ideas and was looking forward to the prospect of getting finally settled in to the house in Fornalutx.

There you have it, Damian – jobs I have done. Good luck with your search and may you find something you enjoy doing and which brings in adequate cash.

Lots of love,
your loving g'ma
Veronica

Dearest Olivia

It's great news that you and Mark are getting married and I am looking forward to coming to England for your wedding. It's made me think of my own marriage, so very different from yours and how war distorts and complicates human relationships. I met your grandfather, as you may or may not know, in Egypt in 1942. Our first meeting was not particularly significant. I shared a flat with my friend, Rosemary, in Heliopolis, about twenty minutes walk from the Museum on the edge of the desert, where we worked. The Museum was a large, very Eastern looking building with a domed roof and had been intended as a museum for flora and fauna. But it had been commandeered by the British and had become the headquarters of 276 Wing to which we belonged. Although commanded by the RAF it was actually a mixed Services unit owing to the nature of our work. We had a small naval contingent as well as a few military personnel and some ladies from the Foreign Office.

On this particular afternoon Rosemary and I were having our siesta (very necessary in the Cairo heat) when the flat doorbell rang. I was just waking up and feeling a bit grumpy and I wondered who on earth might be ringing the bell at this time of day? When I opened the flat door there on the landing stood a young RAF officer. He was slim and fair with a spectacular handlebar moustache and very blue eyes. There was a small suitcase on the floor by his feet. "I'm sorry to disturb you," he said, "but I've just come out of hospital and I'm sharing this flat opposite to you with another chap but he's not in. I wonder whether I could leave my suitcase with you for an hour or so?" I was just about to say 'no problem.' No, let me correct that, that's not what we said in those days, I would have been about to say 'that won't be a bother' when it struck me that he looked terribly pale and wan, so rather grudgingly I invited him in for a cup of tea.

Rosemary had by now also surfaced and I left her in the sitting room with our unexpected visitor while I went to our cockroach infested kitchen to make a pot of tea. We ventured into the kitchen as little as possible, what with the problems of lighting the spirit stove and the general sense that we did not belong there, it wasn't our territory. But Hassan, our servant, produced culinary marvels from this unpromising area. However he was not around in the afternoons, he disappeared after lunch and we didn't see him again until we returned from work in the evenings. So after a considerable lapse of time I took the tea to the sitting room.

As I had never known anyone who didn't take milk in their tea and it never occurred to me to ask, so when I handed Tom, (as he told us he was called), his cup, he looked slightly embarrassed and said he was afraid he could not drink tea with milk in it. I took his cup back to the kitchen and emptied it down the sink. I was about to pour the tea again into his cup when he stopped me and asked with even greater embarrassment whether I had rinsed the cup otherwise the taste of milk would still be present. Well, I thought, as I trailed back to the kitchen to give the cup a cursory rinse, fancy being married to you!

We found out that he belonged to 276 Wing but we had never seen him around as he had been out in the desert in charge of a listening post and then subsequently in hospital where he had been quite ill with quinsy. He was living with Hugh Waters, who was the boss of our section, a brilliant young graduate from Cambridge who was not perhaps the easiest person to get along with and who, after the war, well after the war, married Rosemary. When we came back from Fornalutx I went with Martin and Fiona to stay with them in their first home, Tickhill Castle, near Doncaster which they leased from the Queen. It was a fascinating place, but oh so cold!

But back in hot Cairo it was a little time before I saw Tom again to speak to. For the time being he was back in headquarters, in the Museum and I was vaguely aware of seeing him now and again padding round the Museum with files under his arm or hearing his mellifluous voice through open doors, but apart from that I never gave him another thought. Then one day we happened to coincide in the mess. I was sitting drinking a beer at the end of the morning before walking back to the flat for lunch, and he came and joined me.

The Museum was built on a raised piece of ground and was a great hunk of a building and with its domed roof looked very impressive right on the edge of the desert and overlooking the Cairo-Alexandria road. I think it cannot have been quite finished when the British took it over because it lacked steps up to the entrance and we had a makeshift set of wooden steps which were perfectly adequate but not in keeping with the rest of the building. The mess was a low single-storied concrete building several yards away, in front of the Museum. You had to cross an expanse of sand to get there and when the *khamseen* blew the sand stung your face. I remember one of the Foreign Office ladies, Scottish she was, remarking "it's a nice wee warrm wind." That wasn't my opinion of it! The mess provided drinks and snacks but not really a proper meal. All officers and civilians who were stationed at the Museum lived out, either in flats or boarding houses. The chaps, as the other ranks were affectionately known as, had their own quarters tucked away behind the Museum.

In wartime people sometimes find that they are square pegs in round holes and this is what happened to Tom when he arrived in Egypt in the spring of 1941. In Britain he had been an intelligence officer, debriefing bomber crews on their return from a raid. He had volunteered for overseas service and had expected to be employed in something fairly similar, but he was not going to a specific post. On his troopship was a certain

Wing Commander who was to be the commanding officer of the new 276 Wing being set up at the Museum in Heliopolis. Tom had a happy knack of getting on well with all sorts of people, his unassuming charm endeared him to many from different backgrounds. He was no sycophant but he was always popular with his senior officers, just as he was with his peer group, not to mention the other ranks who not infrequently brought him their personal problems for advice and help. It was this quality which probably made him such a good teacher of photography later on in life. Anyway when they all arrived in Egypt, the Wing Commander said to the powers-that-be, "I want this man in my unit," and Tom was duly posted to 276 Wing. It hadn't been taken into account that he knew no German and that his knowledge of radio was no greater than the rest of the population who owned portable Pye sets! He was sent out into the desert to set up one of the first new listening posts and he told me subsequently that if it hadn't been for his NCO he would have been in a pickle. Nothing disastrous happened and then he became ill with tonsillitis leading to quinsy.

We went out a couple of times and he revealed to me that he was married, in fact at the time of his overseas posting his marriage was only six months old. I asked him why he had volunteered when he could have waited until he was sent. "I suppose because I'm a selfish sod," was his reply, "and the world beckoned." But he never thought it would have happened so quickly. When the event overtook them they were both very upset but once something is set in motion in war there's no chance to change your mind.

And so I continued to accept other invitations and fight off unwanted advances in taxis coming home late at night from Cairo. There was a great dearth of British women in Cairo or should I say a vast presence of British men – HQ types and men back on short leaves from the desert front. Women could pick and choose and not a few went for the top brass, friendship with a colonel brought more perks than friendship with a subaltern and of course there was all the glamour of reflected rank. In the melting pot that was Cairo many strange and varied liaisons bubbled and some were forged to last beyond the war, others came to an abrupt end. Of course we were not the only women around, there were plenty of beautiful Egyptian women, only language and culture made it almost impossible for any British man to get to know them. The exceptions were those who were actresses or film stars and it was not unusual to find them at various parties. A friend of ours had a very beautiful Syrian girl friend but he was, I think, an exception.

It wasn't long before Hugh and Tom moved out of the flat opposite and took up residence in a small villa on the edge of the desert and within sight of the Museum. By now Tom's convalescent light duties were coming to an end and a job would have to be found for him. The obvious move would have been to post him to another unit but the C.O. wanted to hang on to him. Then unexpectedly the Messing Officer was posted to other duties. The Wingco got what he wanted and Tom became 276 Wing's Messing Officer. He moved into a tiny cell-like office in the officers' mess, next door to the Accountancy Officer, so I could no longer observe his feline tread around the Museum or chance to hear his voice through some open door.

He was responsible for the running and provisioning of all three messes – the officers, the sergeants and the airmen. The bulk of the provisions came from the NAAFI but fresh food, such as vegetables and fruit, was bought from local Egyptian suppliers and Arab merchants. Tom tried to supply as much fresh food as possible for the sergeant's and airmen's messes and he was good at bargaining and not likely to be diddled. He enjoyed it, knew a little Arabic, was good tempered and had a sense of humour so he got along with the Arabs (or wogs, as the troops called them). I was told that it stood for well dressed oriental gentleman(?). I recently looked up 'wog' in the dictionary and it didn't tell me much more. 'Offensive remark to non-white person. 20th century. Origin unknown.'

Tom's biggest bugbear was the accounts and those had to be audited by the Accountancy Officer every two months. He was a thin-lipped taciturn Scot without much humour and I think he disapproved of Tom in general and his accounting in particular. Anyway every so often Tom couldn't get his books to balance and the deficit had to come out of his own pocket, fortunately it was never very much.

A considerable amount of entertaining went on at Hugh and Tom's villa and Rosemary and I, along with others, were invited to parties there. Hugh not only had a very active intellect but was musically gifted as well. He had a good voice and played the guitar, which he took up professionally after the war. Tom also had a very melodious tenor voice (he had sung in the church choir all his youth) and the two of them would sing opera, with Hugh at the piano, for the entertainment of their guests and just for the fun of it. Although at home I had heard opera on the radio and had gone with my mother to endless orchestral concerts in Edinburgh, I had never actually seen an opera nor did I know much about it. My first real experience of opera was to be when we were in Italy, when I heard Puccini's Tosca in Bari. Tom had a number of records of opera which he played me on a wind-up gramophone.

Tom was just that bit older than many of the other young officers. He may not have been so highly educated (he never went to university) as they were, but his life experience outstripped theirs. They often consulted him, both about their love life and more mundane matters. He also had an extensive and eclectic knowledge of literature and poetry absorbed during those long empty evenings in the Australian outback. He preferred the company of those younger men than some of the older ones although of course there was no rigid pattern, but he liked their lively minds and found them more in keeping with his own.

Tom was a socialist and I had never come across a socialist before, my father and mother voted conservative I'm sure, but politics was never really discussed in our home. I could see that

Tom was much more of a rebel than I was ever likely to be and he had some opinions I had never heard voiced before. (When we moved to Newdigate, he was asked to be secretary of the local Labour Party but he very soon got fed up with it and resigned. He wasn't really seriously political, his interests lay in artistic pursuits.)

I ended up working with a young Flight Lieutenant called Cecil Gould. He was very tall, rather like a stork and when he got cross he would thump his fist against his waist. He often got cross with Tom who teased him and he would thump his fist and say "oh stop it, Tom, stop it" in his rather high-pitched voice. He was known (affectionately) as Girlie Gould. Nothing much was spelled out in those days but we all knew. He and I were incarcerated in a curious small glass office within the big office where all the rest of the section worked. It was a form of extra security as we were working on Ultra material. Cecil was an extremely clever young man and had a profound knowledge of art, and after the war he joined the National Gallery staff where he worked until his retirement. During his last five years he was Keeper and Deputy Director. We lost touch with him after the war but I always had news of him from Hugh and Rosemary right up until his death in 1994, as they remained friends.

Tom and I saw a fair bit of one another. We sometimes went riding early in the morning before breakfast. He would come and collect me in a taxi about 6 a.m. and we would drive to the stables which were some way out of Heliopolis and then we rode across the desert. The horses were tricky brutes with mouths like iron and Tom liked to get them going, I think principally to see if I was scared (which I was but tried not to show it) and they galloped off at great speed. We usually ended up quite near the Museum from where the groom collected them and took them back to the stables and we walked back to our respective dwellings for breakfast. Rosemary thought I was mad, horses were not her thing and she didn't believe in getting up any earlier than necessary.

So then… Tom began to press for more than just friendship. I resisted. I had not been brought up to go off with another woman's husband. He was persistent and I was becoming more and more deeply attracted to him. Then he told me of the agreement he and his wife had made when they realised that they would be apart most probably for a very long time. They had agreed that should either of them meet someone, they should be free to have an affair, that they would tell each other and that it wouldn't make any difference to their marriage. I suppose that can be seen as naively idealistic. Life in wartime seemed fragile and fleeting, even if one were not on the battlefield. The future was a blur, the present, the here and now was what was important and there was an impatient desire to seize experience before it eluded you. But I was still not sure. I couldn't quite square it with my conscience. Tom was patient and persistent. Then, Mary, his wife, briefly befriended a forlorn Polish soldier and Tom said he minded more than he had expected. Her 'infidelity' was fleeting but it provided the kick-start for me to become the cause of Tom's infinitely more substantial unfaithfulness. After three months I caved in. I argued with myself that as Tom would return to his wife after the war, it would be me who would get hurt and nobody else. The choice was mine and I had made it. 'After the war' – that mythical country that all of us talked about and none of us knew what its topography would be like.

I found Egypt such a strange exotic mixture of noises and smells and people, of poverty and wealth, of the indigenous population and swarms of foreigners both civilian and military who thronged the streets. Since the Romans, Egypt had been a country almost entirely dominated by foreign powers and with the opening of the Suez Canal by the French in 1869 it became a country of strategical importance. From the end of the nineteenth century until 1922 when Egypt gained its independence, it was dominated by Britain and even afterwards there was still a strong British influence. Our friend Mahmoud Taher el Araby whom Tom got to know before I arrived in

Cairo, told us many interesting things about the politics of Egypt. He had been imprisoned for twelve years by the British for attempting to assassinate Kitchener during the First World War.

When we knew him he had become very pro-British and had a job at the Embassy as a sort of propaganda agent. After his release from prison he was instrumental in effecting various prison reforms through his journalism and influence with some politicians. He was such a nice man, kind and helpful and spoke excellent English. We went to a couple of parties on his flat roof above his Cairo flat and it was there that I saw a belly dancer for the first time. Tom and I were also invited to lunch on our own and introduced to his wife although she did not eat with us. I think I was regarded as an honorary man because I wore uniform!

Towards the end of October 1942 what came to be known as The Great Flap happened. The Germans were practically at the gates of Alexandria. Rommel was making what appeared to be an unstoppable advance. We couldn't hear the gunfire from Cairo but it was heard by people living in Alexandria. The Egyptians were preparing to welcome the new army of occupation and probably had swastika flags stashed away ready to bring out once the Brits were gone. The order had come through that we were to prepare for evacuation and that all top secret documents and sensitive material were to be burned. Charred pieces of paper floated down onto the streets of Cairo around headquarters. At the back of the Museum an incinerator was set up and we all brought file-fulls of information to be burned; the smell was quite sick making. We were told to pack one small suitcase and bring it up to the mess along with our camp beds and tin hats. Nobody knew anything and we were told nothing. As in most crises rumour was rife – we were retreating to Luxor, we were going to Eritrea, but nobody knew anything not even our C.O., or so he said. All work came to a halt, we just sat around the mess playing cards, reading and intermittently chewing sandwiches and drinking. Tom was the only one who was busy, keeping up a constant supply of food and drink. Rosemary and I were due to pay our next month's rent on the flat, but we held back until we knew whether we would still be in occupation. This caused endless shrieks and moans from our Egyptian landlady when she saw us leave with our little suitcases. "Yes of course, Madame, we'll pay if we come back but there is a war on, you know." We didn't want to pay for some Wehrmacht officer who might become Madame's tenant in our place. Our landlady was the wife of a colonel in the Egyptian army. He was a tall, quiet man who looked like a kindly wolf and who often came up from their ground floor flat to apologize and smooth things over after we had had a complaining visit from his bracelet jingling wife.

After two or three days of this unsettling life the miracle did happen. The Eighth Army commanded by Montgomery halted Rommel's advance and the German forces were held at El Alamein and very soon were being pushed back. It was of course wonderful news and was the turning point of the war but from a personal point of view it was a bit of an anti-climax. We had to unpack all the files we had been going to take with us and start getting back down to work again and after all the excitement of the possible retreat it was hard. For months afterwards, whenever anything was mislaid or could not be found, the comment was always the same – "oh that was burned in the Great Flap."

Rosemary and I returned to our flat in the Sharia Champollion, down by the racecourse, and duly paid our month's rent in advance, Madame was mollified and more friendly now that we were no longer the losers. Life trundled on as usual. Regretfully we had to get rid of Hassan who was such a good cook but he was diddling us shamefully and there was nothing we could do about it. When we confined him to a precise amount of money to buy food for lunch one day, we came back from work and the table was unlaid and Hassan was sulking in the kitchen. "Money too little – no possible buy lunch." Our next *safragi* was Sudanese. Abdul was infinitely more honest but not such a good cook and with very little English, but we got along. Then the time came when Rosemary and I gave up the flat and went our separate ways. She to her army captain, also stationed at the Museum, and who like Tom was married but did return, I think successfully, to his wife after the war. I went to live at the villa with Tom, and Hugh. It was a sweet little house and had a garden with a lovely mimosa tree and there was a veranda running all round the bottom part of the house which looked out across the desert. For me the rent was cheaper than the flat had been because it was shared between three.

Winter in Egypt was not particularly comfortable. It could be quite chilly. We changed into our blue uniforms around November. The Museum was very cold and draughty and I would often work wrapped up in an army blanket. The villa could be chilly in the evening but it had a small brick fireplace and sometimes we made a fire with dried camel dung. Of course there were beautiful days as well but like most hot countries no provision was made to deal with colder weather. Tom and I began to get a bit fidgety about living with Hugh in the villa. It was fine, the three of us got along perfectly well but Tom and I were a bit tired of the endless entertaining and parties etc. not to mention the fact that it was quite expensive as our *safragi* had to be given extra money for party food and paid for working longer hours. Hugh seemed oblivious to expense.

One evening when he was talking about the next party he thought we should have Tom protested mildly and Hugh looked at us in disgust and said – God, you two are just like a married couple! So eventually after Christmas we moved out to a flat of our own not very far from the villa. There were no hard feelings. Hugh continued to live in the villa by himself and enjoy his active social life unhampered by reluctant housemates. His parents had died in a car crash when he was a young teenager and he was brought up by a male guardian whom he didn't particularly like and had gone to boarding school. From quite an early age he had control of the money his parents had left him and spent it lavishly. He really was a character larger than life and it was so sad when many, many years later I visited him in the Maudsley hospital in London after a severe breakdown, to see him so diminished, a ghost of his former self, sitting motionless, staring at his hands. But he did eventually get better and whenever I visited the UK from Fornalutx, I would go and stay with him and Rosemary.

Our flat wasn't wonderful, it was on the ground floor and quite small, but we did appreciate being on our own and able to do what we wanted. We had a rather ancient *safragi* but he was a pleasant fellow and his cooking was adequate. It was a change to get home from work and just relax, listen to music on Tom's wind-up gramophone or read and Tom often used to read me poetry and tell me about his life in Australia and how frustrating he had found it. Sometimes in the afternoons during siesta time on days when it wasn't too hot, we would get on our bikes and cycle along the path beside the Sweet Water Canal (which was far from sweet) and go to visit our potter friend.

Hassan was very different from Taher and lived in a tiny windowless shack but he was mostly out of doors on his kick wheel. He was a very fine potter and as well as pots he made interesting masks. We bought quite a lot of his work as did others from the Museum. It was a nice little excursion and he always insisted we drink Turkish coffee with him.

I was 23 and Tom was 33 and he knew much more about life than I did, although I never felt he was that much older than me. I had never been particularly interested in boys of my own age anyway and was more drawn to someone whose experience was greater than my own. Eventually Tom told his wife what was going on and she was predictably very upset. I wrote her a letter to try and reassure her but I can't now remember whether she replied because my memory of the letter she wrote me when Tom died remains uppermost in my mind. After that we corresponded intermittently. By then Mary was married to her second husband who worked for the British

Council and they were in Egypt and more or less covering the same ground as Tom and I had done. Mary was a very generous spirited person. The fact that she re-married and also had four children was a salve to my conscience.

I saw so much more of the Middle East with Tom than I would ever have done on my own. There were places where women could go on their own but mostly where there were other Europeans around. On the whole people were not very adventurous on their leaves, Alexandria was the most usual choice or sometimes a deserted beach resort where they could just relax. Tom and I had three wonderful holidays during the time we were in Egypt. The first one we went on was to Syria and Lebanon in September 1942. We travelled by train, by bus, by bicycle and Shanks' pony (on foot, to you). We visited Damascus and Beirut and the Cedars of Lebanon, trees so big and strong and sweet smelling. That was part of the journey we did on foot. We arrived at this tiny village on bicycles which we had hired in a small town about seven miles away down a roughish track. The owner of the bicycles said it would be all right to leave them at the village, somebody would bring them back.

We were given quite a welcome when we arrived, I suspect the bicycle man must have alerted the village somehow. We were offered a bed for the night and a meal. My Arabic was non-existent, Tom's was primitive but there was one man who spoke amazing English. They prepared a wonderful feast of roast lamb and couscous, vegetables and fruit and then we all sat down in a big circle on the ground and helped ourselves with our hands. Several onlookers hovered outside the circle and I felt rather bad that they were not partaking of the feast. The women were in evidence, wreathed in smiles and serving ice cold water from terracotta jugs into our clay cups. I wondered later on if the village might have been Christian. We were to spend the night in a small single-storied dwelling, in fact it was hardly more than an oval shaped room with a beaten earth floor and it had a curious, high curved ceiling which was

163

tiled on the exterior, making it look rather like a chapel from the outside. There were no windows, just a door. In the middle of the room stood a high, smallish double bed made up with spotless white embroidered bed linen. It looked inviting after quite a tiring day and we sank into a soft feathery mattress. We hadn't been in bed for more than five minutes when Tom said he was getting bitten and I realised that I was too. Bed bugs were no rarity in Cairo and Rosemary and I had had to get our mattresses fumigated, but here in the country in such a spotless looking bed it was unexpected. We stood it for as long as we could but in the end had to get up and unroll our sleeping bags and settle down for the rest of the night on the earth floor. It was not very comfortable and even on the floor we got the odd bite, probably fleas. We didn't of course say anything in the morning and the bed looked as if it had been slept in.

We thanked our hosts, settled the bill which was surprisingly modest and set off up the mountain to the Cedars. It was quite a climb and although the weather was nice to begin with, it started to rain and was chilly at the top. We did not linger very long around the Cedars because we had been told that a little way down on the other side was an hotel and we were damp and tired. Luckily we had not been misinformed. We came upon the hotel from the rear and when we went round to the front it looked like some big Swiss chalet perched on the hillside. It was open and what's more it had HOT water! We were lucky because it was the end of the season and the hotel was about to shut for the winter, there were no other guests. We had a bug-less night and a long deep sleep. We were back on a proper road again and so the next morning we phoned for a taxi to take us back to civilisation.

Our next port of call was Baalbeck. Tom had been to Baalbeck before on a previous leave by himself, before I arrived in Cairo, and had spent most of his time painting. This time he had a camera and took photographs. On his previous visit he had made friends with Fawzi who was in charge of the mounted patrol which policed the surrounding area. We went in search of him and found him, he gave Tom a great welcome. We stayed in a small, rather chilly hotel but we got warm by hiring bicycles and exploring, not to mention scrambling about in the impressive ruins. Fawzi took us riding on the beautiful horses belonging to the mounted patrol, they were mostly stallions but mercifully I was given a docile mare. He spoke French which made communication much easier. On our last evening he invited us to his house for a meal. His wife was very sweet and very shy and only spoke Arabic so we couldn't communicate very much except smile, but it was a happy evening. We left the next day and travelling by bus and hitching, got back to Cairo quite late in the evening and were back on duty at the Museum the following morning.

Our next long leave was to Palestine in the spring of 1943. It was so wonderful to see the orange and lemon groves and the colour of the burgeoning wild flowers after the aridity of the Egyptian countryside. Egypt had its own beauty but Palestine was something different. I always remember the wonderful smell of the orange blossom wafting into the back of the open lorry on which we had hitched a lift just as the dawn was breaking. We went nearly everywhere including three days in Jerusalem and a visit to the Dead Sea which I found singularly unattractive. It was a very hot day and there were clouds of potash dust swirling about from the nearby potash works. I believe there is now a very grand hotel and the whole area has been smartened up.

When we got home again to Heliopolis we decided we were going to put the two holidays together and write a book about them, which we did. It was called 'Middle East Hitchhike', we both worked on the text and it was illustrated with Tom's photos. We did actually finish it and Tom designed a cover but by the time we started to look for a publisher, the war was over and there had been a surfeit of war books so it never saw the light of day.

We decided to move flats as we had had a couple of break-ins. Being on the ground floor it was all too easy for intruders.

We didn't lose a great deal – Tom, his gold cuff links and me some expensive made-to-measure items of silk underwear. Cairo was a great place for made-to-measure clothes. You could hardly buy anything off the hook. Anyway, we moved to a much nicer first floor flat with a big balcony and a grand piano. We shared it with a colleague from the Museum. Richard Blackham, a rather nervous, musical young man, whose piano playing gave us a lot of pleasure. It was in this flat that Tom acquired Slimey. He bought him off a snake charmer and was assured that he was harmless. No doubt he was but I did not take to him, I did not share Tom's affinity with snakes and when he used to toss him on to the bed just as I was waking up from my siesta, I usually screamed. Mercifully he disappeared quite soon, slithering off somewhere else.

It was the very last leave we had in the autumn of 1943 when we travelled three days by camel to the monastery of St. Catherine in the wilderness of Sinai, which surpassed everything. Ever since arriving in Egypt it had been an ambition of Tom's to undertake this journey. He was fascinated by St. Catherine's and had read quite a lot about it as well as about journeys made there by other travellers It was an expedition that required a great deal of pre-preparation. Tom made countless trips into central Cairo to be interviewed by the Greek Orthodox archbishop and finally to obtain the written permits allowing us to stay at the monastery. Then there was the question of getting to El Tor on the Gulf of Suez where we would hire the camels to take us inland. Through various contacts and conversations with Egyptian acquaintances, we hit on the idea of booking passages on the boat which went down the Gulf monthly, visiting all the lighthouses and bringing provisions, mail, changes of personnel, investigating officials etc. This, as so much in Egypt, was fraught with delays, mistakes and misunderstandings, but everything did actually come together a couple of days before we were due to leave. The other aspect of this journey was that it was out of bounds. In theory all personnel on leave had to be contactable by phone

– at least eventually – and that was not something which could apply to our little jaunt. So we only told our closest friends where we were going and swore them to secrecy.

Finally we scrambled aboard the Diesel, fast train to Suez, with two suitcases, one of clothes and one of provisions, and our sleeping bags. The voyage down the Gulf was most intriguing. The Captain of the S.S. *Aida* was an interesting man, a devout Moslem and he was most kind to us. We took our meals with him in his cabin along with an architect and an engineer, both Egyptian but speaking very good English. He allowed us to go ashore in the motor launch at the lighthouses and so we saw what went on each month when the ship called and how pleased the lighthouse keepers were to receive their mail and other goodies and have a bit of diversion, which we certainly caused! Not far from one of the lighthouses was a unit of the Desert Patrol. They had these wonderful racing camels and we were given a ride. But it was no preparation for what was to come. The Desert Patrol camels had beautiful leather saddles with a sheepskin thrown over them and their gait was smooth and rhythmic. The camels we hired at El Tor were skinny beasts and the saddles were made of wood and stuffed sacking, held together by string.

It took us two days and three nights to reach El Tor where we arrived just after breakfast. Our immediate requirements were seen to by the *Mamur* who was the headman of the village, you could describe him as a very overworked Mayor. He collected taxes and fines, arbitrated disputes, answered everyone's queries and complaints, in fact his office seemed a sort of social club where those who had nothing much to do (and they seemed quite plentiful) sat around drinking coffee, smoking and chatting. Anyway he was courtesy itself and took us in his battered old car to the El Tor monastery where there was a monk who seemed to be expecting us. We were refreshed with *zibib* or *arak* as it is more commonly known as, and fresh figs. Then we were taken through the courtyard to scrubland at the back in order to inspect the camels. They were a fairly mangy lot and one we discarded as it didn't look as if it could cross the street let alone the Sinai desert. After a great deal of coming and going and sitting down in the shade and eating grapes, we finally ended up with three passable camels, one was for the baggage and the water, carried in goatskin bags, and the other two for us to ride. There were more delays while the baggage camel was loaded and the rope broke and more had to be found, but finally in the late afternoon we were on our way across the rippling sand towards the towering mountains in the distance, turning dark blue as evening approached. We were accompanied by the camel man, who was also our guide, a teenage lad and two younger boys.

It took us eight days to travel there and back, spending three days at the monastery. It was an awe inspiring experience, both in the journeying along the *wadis* between massive mountains whose colouring changed throughout the day, sleeping on hard stony ground beneath a canopy of stars and stirring in the sharp, cool mornings at our guide's early morning call of *ya hawagg,* and then sharing in the daily life of the monastery. I may say that we walked more of the way than we rode on the camels!

The monastery, which was founded by the Emperor Justinian in 500 A.D., was like a self-contained village. Apart from their religious duties, every monk could turn his hand to some secular trade or artistic skill. The bishop, an endearing old gentleman with a long snowy white beard, spoke French and typed away on his Remington typewriter. (I am sure that the present incumbent is busy sending e-mails on his computer.) When we were there they were building a new wing to house more guest rooms and a huge new library, but progress was slow because of the war and scarcity of materials. We were happy to be the only guests and appreciated the calm, peaceful atmosphere in this dramatic setting, such a happy contrast to the noise and clamour of Cairo. I believe that nowadays coachloads of tourists descend on the monastery down a well-engineered tarmac road and I can imagine how that must have changed the ambience.

When we got back to El Tor, we found we had missed the boat, the S.S. *Aida* had sailed the previous afternoon. The *Mamur* said not to worry, there was a motor launch taking fish to Suez due any day now and in the meantime he settled us in the Rest House which was equipped with bedding and crockery and had a shower. We still had four days of leave left so we weren't that bothered and El Tor was a pleasant place to laze about in. We drank mint tea with the doctor who had a smattering of English and fished for our supper which we grilled on a fire on the beach and ate on the Rest House veranda, watching the sun set. Nevertheless we started to scan the horizon somewhat anxiously for this boat that never appeared. With one and a half days to go we consulted the *Mamur* and he suggested that he took us in his own car. But he could not do it without authorisation from the Governor of Sinai and suggested we sent a telegram, which we did but got no reply. In the meantime we heard of a contractor's car that was going to Suez the next day. The *Mamur* was not keen for us to go with the contractor as he had had two accidents but with no reply to our telegram there was no alternative and we had a very uncomfortable, bumpy hot drive to Suez and arrived just in time to catch the evening Diesel back to Cairo.

So, dear Livvy, I expect you think all my wartime service in Egypt was spent going on exotic journeys. Not so. In the twenty-four months I spent there I had six weeks leave plus the few days when I went on my own to Luxor just before leaving for Italy. We worked hard, never less than eight hours a day, seven days a week with 48 hours off every month. The work was often tedious, leafing through endless log sheets of routine German wireless traffic until one spotted something unusual, a new code word, unusual repetitions indicating that some new move or strike was afoot, or some fresh re-grouping of forces. It certainly required alertness to recognise the need when to pass the information upwards.

But that's enough for now, you don't need to hear any more of your grandma's wartime reminiscing. Let me know what date the wedding is going to be and I'll book my flight.

Much love

G'ma Veronica

Dearest Alex

So you're back from your trip to Lapland. I hope you found Father Christmas well and not too upset by the lack of snow. How exciting going to see him in his own home. I just had to picture him in my imagination but I was always very pleased when he drank the sherry and ate the sponge cake put out to refresh him after his exertions of climbing down the chimney. You certainly go to some exciting places.

I wonder what you would think of the holidays I had when I was a child? Not much, I don't suppose. I loved them and thought they were quite magical. We always went away for two months in the summer and then there were the Easter holidays, usually two weeks. But the Easter holidays had no special remembered magic, we usually went near Edinburgh, sometimes to the seaside. I remember picnics crouching in the lee of sand dunes, trying to shelter from a chilly wind and the sea looking grey and unfriendly. We stayed in rather uncomfortable boarding houses – rooms with attendance was what they were known as. Apart from one Easter at Moffat which is inland and south of Edinburgh, I don't remember much. But Moffat had a park which contained a large pond or small lake where they rented canoes and I spent most of the fortnight paddling about and exploring the inlets. I suppose it was very tame fun but I wasn't really in Moffat, in my imagination I was in much more exciting waters in some mysterious location.

But the summer holidays – now, they were something quite different. Throughout my childhood and into my mid teens my parents rented houses in the Highlands of Scotland for about eight to ten weeks, the whole of August and most of September with a bit of July tacked on at the beginning. For the period of the school holidays, I suppose. When I was a baby and until I was about seven years old we went to Croftmore near Boat of Garten, a small farm with a longish, cottage-type farmhouse where we installed ourselves while Mr and Mrs Grant and their son George moved into a tiny dwelling. It was not unusual for farmers to move out of their houses in the summer and let them. My memory of Croftmore is fairly hazy and mixed up with anecdotes and stories from the rest of my family, not to mention my father's many photographs (and my mother's sketches). But one thing I do remember is Mrs Grant calling her son to his dinner. George was what today would be described as someone with learning difficulties, we described him as, not the full shilling.

Every day at noon, Mrs Grant would come out of her house, funnel her hands round her mouth, throw back her head and shout: "Garge, Garge, come west tae yer dinner!" Presumably George always worked to the east of the farm. When, in September 2000, my sister Elizabeth and I were on holiday in an hotel in Boat of Garten, we drove to Croftmore and had a nose around. It had now been turned into a riding school and the Grants were in the local graveyard. But the six larch trees which my sister told me my father had planted as a windbreak at the bottom of the garden were now tall, healthy trees and I felt it was fitting remembrance of all those happy summer days our family spent there.

The next summer holidays I remember were on the island of Mull, off the west coast of Scotland. Another farm, owned by the Livingstons, three brothers and one sister, all unmarried. They fetched us from Oban in their big, wide and shallow fishing boat and we sailed straight across to Mull and up Loch Spelvie where the farm was, not far from the lochside. It was a chilly sail from Oban and could be quite rough, I can remember feeling very scared on one of those journeys. I think we went there two years running, maybe three. Much later, during the war, we heard, on what authority I don't know, that the Livingstons had been cattle thieves and that they used their fishing boat to transport the stolen beasts. They were said to have had a collie dog, the centre of whose tongue had been cut out and wired, so that it could not bark and it was very skilled at rounding up the cattle. True or not true, they were very kind to us and there are photos of me standing on the top of hay carts holding one of the brother's hands or astride a big Clydesdale with a brother at the horse's head.

There was quite a lot of boating on the loch and of course, fishing. On fine days Francis and Elizabeth swam. I would try but without success for so many summers. I liked my natty bathing dress but I hated the smell of my rubber bathing cap. I felt cold and was frightened of the water and the stones were slippery and hurt my feet. The other two were pretty good swimmers, they had gone regularly to swimming baths in Edinburgh and been given lessons when they were quite young, and I don't know why I hadn't. Neither of our parents swam so I was reliant on my older siblings to help and encourage me. They did make some effort and kindly led me by the hand between them out to deeper waters and tried to get me swimming, but it was the same as the saying of the horse and the water, the horse can't be made to drink, I couldn't be made to swim. So they got fed up and went off to swim themselves and I waded back tearfully to the shore where my concerned Mama dried my tears and my shivering wet, little body and put me into my clothes again. I liked being *on* the water but not *in* the water.

The upshot was that I did not learn to swim until I was 15. That was at Sherborne School where it was compulsory and I was very embarrassed to be given swimming lessons in the open air swimming pool with girls so much younger than myself. I was always a very indifferent swimmer without any confidence. I had yet to experience climates where the heat made one long to jump into cool water. Scottish lochs are not to be recommended for young nervous children hoping to learn to swim! It wasn't until my retirement that I really started to enjoy swimming and to gain some confidence in the buoyant waters of the Mediterranean. It has been one of the many pleasures of my advanced years.

At the end of the last summer that we were with the Livingstons my mother got a very bad chest infection and couldn't go home with us. We left her in the care of Miss Livingston and ten days later our dad went back and fetched her home. He, of course couldn't spend all summer with us. He usually had about three weeks and then returned for the odd weekend. On holiday, plus fours and a tweed cap replaced his office suit and bowler hat, later substituted by an Anthony Eden. My father never wore the kilt, I suppose as a lowlander he wasn't entitled to, but we children frequently wore kilts, though never after we became teenagers. The only close relative I knew who wore a kilt continuously was my brother-in-law, Tur, Bud's husband.

If being on holiday was exciting, so too was getting there. What must be, I think, my first remembered holiday, (and we were still going to Croftmore then) was when shortly after an early breakfast we were picked up by a horse-drawn cab which accommodated all of us and the luggage, and were driven up the hill and down the hill and along Princes Street to the Waverley Station. But after that it was always an ordinary taxi that called for us and drove us to the station. But I loved the bustle of the station, the hoots of the steam engines and the busy porters with their barrows who took people's luggage and heaved it up onto the racks in the carriages. Then there were the smells I associated with the journey. The fumes from the engine, slightly fusty carriages and our sandwiches, our lovely sandwiches – sardine and hard boiled egg and cress. Francis and Elizabeth usually read or played naughts and crosses but I liked to look out of the window at the passing countryside, in fact I liked to stick my head out of the window on the non corridor side. But I was not allowed to do this when the train was going through a tunnel in case I got a spark in my eye. Our mother always brought tissues with which she cleaned the dust off the windows and ledges and when I went to the lavatory I had to line the seat with lavatory paper. I always managed to get lots of smuts on my face (I suppose those came from leaning out of the window) and my mama would dab them off with her handkerchief moistened by spit.

I think Bella always came with us, not to look after me anymore but to do the cooking, maybe the tablemaid came as well, I don't remember. If she did, then what happened to my father when he was not on holiday with us? I'm sure he couldn't even boil an egg and there were no frozen meals in those days. I expect that he stayed at his club in Princes Street. Later on, much later on, after we had moved to Albert Terrace and I was old enough to stay up for dinner with my parents, he performed a regular little domestic duty every evening when our meal was finished by taking the salt, pepper and mustard pots off the dining room table, putting them on a little wooden tray and returning them to the corner cupboard. Then he would sidle to the dining room door, blow my mother a kiss and nip off into the drawing room where he switched on the wireless and settled down to listen to a variety show. Low brow listening of which my mother disapproved! "Frank, how can you listen to such rubbish," she would say, when she appeared ten minutes later after having washed up the glasses in the upstairs pantry.

My great ambition was to be allowed to wear shorts during the holidays, one of my friends from school showed off about wearing grey flannel boys' shorts and I wanted to do likewise. I was dressed in pretty cotton frocks which very soon got crushed and dirty and I was always having to change, although when the weather got cooler in September I wore a kilt and jersey which I preferred. But to my great joy one summer my mother bought me a pair of grey flannel boys' shorts and I was able to relegate my dresses for 'best'. I think it was the summer we went to a farm in Argyllshire, not far from Oban, I can't remember the name of the farm nor of the people but I do remember the name of the bull – What Care I? He was very fierce and never out much in the fields but was kept tied up in the byre, or cowshed. One evening just before the cows were brought in for the evening milking I had gone to open the cowshed door and what should be coming towards me, head down, along the narrow stone passageway but What Care I. My heart leaped to my mouth and I turned and fled, across the farmyard screaming, "the bull's loose, the bull's loose!" Luckily I had the presence of mind to shut the byre door behind me.

I was old enough now (9 or 10) to be of some use on a farm. I was given the job of going to get the cows for the early morning milking. I liked getting up early so it was no hardship. At first I went with one of the farm hands and then I was allowed to do it by myself. It was a magical feeling to be out alone early on a summer's morning, to feel the cool, thin air on my skin but to know that it portended a warm, sunny day. I felt that I really was a farmer as I brought the cows down the sloping field and shooshed them through the narrow gateway and across the farmyard. I got to know them individually, they were no longer just an anonymous herd of cows, each one had its own character.

It was on this farm that I learned to 'blow' the cream. The milk was put into big shallow enamel pans or basins and left to stand until the cream rose to the top, then the cream was blown by somebody (sometimes me) across the top of the basin to the opposite side where it crinkled up into creamy waves and was scooped off with a saucer and put in the cream can. We blew until all the cream had gone and then the milk was tipped into a milk churn. It was always the women's job and I think only the richest milk was treated in this way. Hygiene did not actually enter into the scheme of things and I thought it was great fun. The cream certainly tasted good on my porridge.

The other happening on this farm which I remember was my poor brother Francis being dragged through the midden by a frisky bullock. I don't quite know what he was doing with it, he had it on a rope and was perhaps taking it from one field to another. Maybe he let the rope go too loose but anyway as they were crossing the farmyard it suddenly put its head down and swerved into the midden or dungheap, charged through it dragging Francis in its wake and liberally bespattering him with this not very choice material!

It was here too that I met my Indian friend. He was a tall, thin man and he used to come to the farm for eggs. He and I got chatting and one day he asked me if I would like to go with him and see where he lived. I said I would but that I would have to ask my Mummy and she of course said no, you can't go on your own. I was disappointed and I also thought it was rather rude but I went and told my friend and he gave a sad little smile and said goodbye.

The next day my mother made some enquiries of the farmer's wife and I hung about listening and heard her reply: "Oh he's a very nice gentleman, your wee lass'll no come to any harm with him, Mrs More." So I was given dispensation and the next time he came to the farm for eggs I said to him "I can come with you today." Off we went, hand in hand, down the farm road for about quarter of an hour then we turned left along a much narrower rougher track. After about another ten minutes we came to a big wooden gate and entered a large garden with walkways and pergolas but in a very neglected state and massively overgrown. The house I seem to remember was a big bungalow, the windows and doors were all open and diaphanous looking curtains were blowing outwards. We went in through the open door to a large room and there on a sofa or chaise longue lay an old lady reading a book, she looked ancient to me but maybe she wasn't that old. I was introduced as Veronica, on holiday at the farm and she looked up from her book and smiled at me. "Would you like some lemonade, dear?" she asked and I said I would. The tall Indian went away to the back of the house and I chatted with the old lady until he returned with a glass of real lemonade made with lemons and two little sponge cakes with pink icing. There was a sort of fairy tale feeling about the place, so different from the farm and all the animals and my own family. It had this air of faint decay over everything, it wasn't obtrusive but it hung there in the atmosphere. When we were walking back to the farm I asked my friend if the lady was his wife. "No," he replied, "she's my employer."

I can't remember whether I made another visit, possibly once. But I do remember Elizabeth saying to my mama that she didn't think I should go off on my own with 'that Indian' and next time she would go with me but it never happened and I think I was glad. It was my own private adventure. On reflection, it was the most incongruous household to find in Argyllshire. I suppose the old lady once lived in India with her husband and was now a widow. But was there any family, had she any children? I never knew. Although we did hear from some source that she died before the war and that her Indian retainer returned to India.

The farm I remember most clearly was near Nethy Bridge, in Speyside. Lettoch was owned by the Macauley family, husband and wife and several children. It was the farm where I did the most 'work'. I was now eleven years old, and for the past year or so I had been having riding lessons in Edinburgh at a stables down Stockbridge run by an ex-cavalry sergeant and I used to enjoy clattering along on the Edinburgh cobbles on our way to the King's Park near Holyrood Palace where we could canter and ride on turf. It was here about a year later that my horse bolted with me and fell, I broke my collar bone. I was thereafter a much more nervous rider. It was at those stables I had my first personal contact with drunkenness. My mother had accompanied me one day to my riding lesson and I was quite frightened to see a strange Mr Dawson lurching about the yard and speaking in a funny slurred voice. This wasn't the Mr Dawson I knew, so calm and reassuring, I thought he was ill. There were only three adults who were going riding and they did not seem bothered. But my mum quickly summed up the situation and said I wouldn't be riding that day. It may have been some day of national or local celebration, I can't remember but I remember being very upset. We watched my riding instructor mount his horse with difficulty and the little mounted group moved off down the street, the end rider giving us a wave and raising her eyebrows expressively. We went back home again and my mother explained to me that Mr Dawson was 'tipsy' and that if you drank too much alcoholic drink it had a bad effect on your body and behaviour. It never happened again and when I went riding next my familiar Mr Dawson was back and that other stranger never reappeared.

In my spare time I used to go down to the stables, only ten minutes walk from Royal Circus, to help groom the horses and 'muck out' the stalls. So this particular summer at Lettoch, I was able to harness the farm cob and put her in the trap. I couldn't manage the Clydesdale because the harness was too heavy and it was so tall but I sometimes succeeded in backing him into the shafts of the cart. At Lettoch I didn't only bring the cows in, I milked them, at least I milked one of them. Fergus, the hired farm labourer, taught me how to spit on the palms of my hands and rub them together so they would slide more easily on the cow's teats. I loved my little three-legged milking stool, I was given a smaller pail which I grasped between my knees and tucking my head against the cow's side, I milked away. I liked the smell of the warm cow and the sound of the milk squirting into the pail. Now and again I would squirt a bit of milk into my own mouth.

This summer we now possessed a motor car – a Wolsey tourer in fawn and dark blue with a folding roof. Before it arrived both my mother and Francis had driving lessons and obtained driving licences. I don't think there were any driving tests in those days, if your driving instructor said you were okay that was it. My father never drove except occasionally from the back seat to the irritation of the driver. The car arrived in the early summer and I remember being taken out for a drive by Francis, we bowled down Stockbridge and round the Botanic Gardens at the breakneck speed of 20 m.p.h. When I was younger I used to look down from my nursery window and watch the two maiden ladies, who lived next door, step into their Austin saloon when their chauffeur brought it round from the garage and see him put a fur rug over their knees on cold days before he drove them off. That, I thought, is what I will have when I am grown up – a car with a chauffeur who puts a rug over my lap. However I was quite chuffed with the Wolsey. Francis was then 18 and two years later Bud learned to drive. Five years later when I learned to drive they had introduced the driving test and my examiner made me stop on the steepest part of the Mound, which snakes up from Princes Street to the High Street, and I had to re-start and was very pleased with myself that I didn't slip backwards one inch!

That summer most of the luggage and the family went north in the car, I went by train with Bella. It was a wonderfully long summer and we stayed on well into September and so I was able to help at the harvest 'stooking', lifting up the sheaves of corn and placing them upright leaning against one another in stooks round the field, usually four to a stook. It was also one of the hottest summers I remember in Scotland and Mrs Macauley provided this wonderfully cooling drink in a smallish milk can. It was cold water into which she put a quantity of very fine oatmeal. We just poured some into a mug whenever we were thirsty and it was amazingly refreshing. I've never ever had it since

I had wonderful freedom and my parents were very unrestrictive. I was expected to join in family picnics which I mostly did and enjoyed, my mother smoking away madly to ward off the midges, or Francis lighting a fire and the smoke getting in my eyes. But if there was something happening at the farm that I wanted to take part in then I was allowed to stay behind. We often had visitors, uncles, aunts and sometimes cousins but I never let them restrict my activities. Aunt Totty visited every summer, by now Granny More was no longer with us and Totty came on her own. If she was in a good mood she was fun but if not she was a blight from which I escaped into the farm. After supper I sometimes played football in the little field next to the house during those long, light evenings with a group of local children mostly a bit older than myself. Bedtime was more elastic than in Edinburgh but by about 9.30 I was usually fetched indoors by one of my siblings and chivvied off upstairs to my bath.

Apart from Fergus, the Macauleys also had a lad working for them. He and Fergus slept in a loft above the hen house. They did have beds, I noted when I went up to see what it was like to sleep in an old hay loft, but there were no sheets, just rather grubby looking blankets. I suppose they ate with the family but where they performed their ablutions or answered the calls of nature is anyone's guess. The lad was called Rob, he was older than me, probably about 13 or 14, very skinny and white faced. He always wore a cloth cap, I never saw him without it even when we were playing football in the evening. He had quite the dirtiest ears I've ever seen, they seemed to be packed with mud and I wondered if he could grow potatoes in them. Anyway he fell in love with me although I didn't know it until after I got back to Edinburgh. He sent me what I suppose were love letters, he could write – just – but he could not spell – at all. It was like working out a code and because I remembered what his speech was like, I managed to get the gist. However it was not a romance that prospered although I did reply to his letters. Poor Rob, I wonder what happened to him. I expect he got called up in the war, perhaps his ears got cleaned and he got a little education and his prospects broadened or maybe he left his spirit on one of the many battlefields. Who knows?

On that same holiday which Bud and I had in September 2000, we went to visit Lettoch. We could see from where we had parked the car a little way off that the house was occupied. Wandering up the still unmade road to the front of the house we saw in the garden an old man picking runner beans. We paused by the garden gate and said good evening to him and Elizabeth told him who we were. His face lit up and he said he could well remember us, he had been a boy of 14 when we were there all those decades ago and remembered me playing football and Francis going fishing.

He had taken the farm over from his father, his wife had died but he had married children who often visited him. The farm had become very much reduced, there were now only a few sheep and hens and he had someone to look after them as he said he could not now do very much apart from looking after himself. We got the impression that his children wanted him to go and live with one of them but he did not want to leave Lettoch. He would have talked all evening and wanted to invite us in but we were at the end of the day and had to get back to the hotel for our supper at Boat of Garten which was not all that near, so we had to leave him. Before we drove off I went to take a look at the farm steadings. The big iron gate was closed on the empty farmyard, the byre, the stables stood empty and silent and as I looked over the gate at the clean concrete pit where once the midden had been, I could see the ghost of that small girl, my former self, who had been so happily engaged in multifarious farm tasks. The following year Elizabeth received a letter from John Macauley's daughter in Aberdeen to say that her father had died and how much our visit the previous summer had meant to him and had furnished him with a subject for conversation ever since. His family were happy he hadn't had to go into hospital and had died at Lettoch which was what he had wanted.

When we returned to Edinburgh after these long summers, I felt this sense of loss and homesickness for several days. I'd mooch around my playroom not knowing what to do with myself. Yes, it was nice to see my friends again but I hadn't really missed them. It was curious really that I who was brought up in a city and mainly had an urban childhood had such a strong affinity with the country and country life and I think it has stayed with me. It was not that I disliked cities, I found them exciting and stimulating and I lived and worked in London for over twenty years, (as well as during the Blitz) but I eventually got myself a cottage in rural Wiltshire to escape to at the weekends. Now in my eighties, cities hold little charm for me, tiring and confusing, and that's why I am very content to live in a semi rural backwater in one of the most beautiful valleys in the world.

But back in those early years before I had reached my teens I seriously missed my farming friends when we came back home. In order to comfort myself, I would emulate some of their habits. Usually when my mother was home I would have tea with her in the afternoon in the drawing room, but if she was out or otherwise engaged, my tea was put in the dining room and I would have it by myself. On those occasions I would pour the tea from my cup into the saucer and make lots of supping noises, then I would cut myself great chunks of bread, butter and jam and stuff them into my mouth and swirl them around with sips of tea from the saucer. Food and liquid in the mouth at the same time was frowned upon as being impolite – so I enjoyed those solitary teas. I was also interested in spitting which was quite a common occurrence on the farm.

I now walked to school every morning on my own, Bud having finished with St. Monica's and gone to the Mount School in York, so I used to practise spitting in a quiet street on my way. (I don't quite know why we two girls were sent away to boarding school and Francis wasn't, he was educated at the Edinburgh Academy. I think it had something to do with our parents' anxiety about homosexual activity at boys' boarding schools. When he went to Oxford Francis found that nearly all his contemporaries had been to public schools and I think he felt at a disadvantage and resented the fact that he had not been sent to one.) Anyway he was much too old and grand to have anything much to do with me at this moment in my life but he would have been very cross if he had seen his little sister spitting on her way to school. I remember there were notices at the tram stops in Edinburgh which said Spitting Spreads Disease, eventually they disappeared as people became more hygiene conscious. I didn't come across spitting again in any significant way until I landed in my first billet of the war in

Dalmeny and then decades later in the eighties when I visited China, where they spat during the opera (but into spitoons).

After we moved from Royal Circus to Albert Terrace which was at the beginning of the 1930s, I don't remember us going to farms anymore. My father rented larger, grander houses, but still in the Highlands of course. I think the reason was that Francis, now at Oxford, wanted to invite his friends and Elizabeth, at the Mount, likewise.

There was always some pony to keep me happy and of course by now I had Freuchie. He was a cairn terrier who was given to me after my many requests for a dog. I was about ten years old and we were still living in Royal Circus when he arrived from Ross-shire after what must have been for him a terrifying train journey shut into a crate. He was delivered on a summer's evening and we took him in the crate down to the drying green. When we slid open the door he shot out and disappeared into the gathering gloom and I thought I had lost him but luckily the walls were without holes and the door at the end was firmly closed.

Eventually he came to me but he had been deeply traumatised by his journey and I can't really think why my parents got a dog from so far away. Perhaps some doggy person whom they consulted must have recommended those particular kennels. Once he got over the journey we soon made friends and I spent hours in Royal Circus gardens, to which we had a key, training him so that on the whole he was fairly obedient. He was very highly strung and when startled could snap at someone, but he was an intelligent dog with a sweet enquiring little face and the whole family grew very fond of him, particularly my Dad who used to tease him sometimes by squirting the skin of a tangerine at his nose when he sat on the armchair near the dining room table when we were having dinner. Freuchie would twitch his nose, shake his little head and look questioningly at my father. I won a couple of prizes with him at agricultural shows. It was when I was in Cairo during the war that he died of a heart attack, aged thirteen years.

I was about 11 or 12 when we left Royal Circus and moved to 12 Albert Terrace, in Morningside on the south side of Edinburgh. It was a semi-detached stone-built house with a garden, front and back which was nice for Freuchie (and me) – I could turn him out into the garden if I couldn't be bothered to take him out. The garden sloped slightly from the front to the back so the lower ground floor was semi basement at the front where the kitchen was but at the back, facing south, it had a clear outlook on the garden. Unlike Royal Circus in north Edinburgh, Albert Terrace was an elevated site and ran along the top ridge of a hill which wound its way gently up from Princes Street and then plunged down again before ascending once more towards the Braid Hills. Gone were these long dark stairs of number 4, instead wide, shallow stairs with a big window half way up led to a roomy, square landing off which opened our four bedrooms. I had the smallest, north facing and rather dark but it was cheerily decorated with orange and green flowery wallpaper and I think orange paintwork. The bathroom which also opened off the landing was tiny and absolutely freezing in winter, not even the steam from the bath seemed to warm it up and of course there was no heating.

I missed my lovely big playroom but I soon got used to the new surroundings and what I really liked was the revolving wooden summerhouse in the back garden. It was a solid contraption but light enough for me to be able to push it round on my own. Sometimes on a warm summer's night I would sleep out there on the chaise longue which my mother used. I'm sure Bella must have been delighted with the move, leaving behind those antediluvian kitchen quarters and that dismal bedroom looking out on the area steps. The Albert Terrace kitchen was small and cosy but not too small. Bella had a brand new gas cooker which must have been a relief after the labour intensive range although she always said her meat roasting was never as good in the gas oven. There was an anthracite stove for warmth. The bedroom was a good sized square room, bright and sunny with a nice garden outlook but she still had to share it with whichever house-tablemaid we had at the time. It wasn't until just before the war that Bella took full possession of her domain, when we ceased to have any other live-in domestic. She remained with my parents until my father died in 1952 but when my mother moved from Albert Terrace to a small flat, there was no room and she had to leave. She became a companion to a rich old lady who left her a legacy which helped in her retirement, spent with a niece in Falkirk. When I was staying with Bud in Perth in the 1980s we visited her there and that was the last time I saw her before she died.

To revert to those summer houses. They were different from the farms and my holidays became more family orientated as I grew up. There were two houses which I remember very clearly. One was called Milltown of Lesmurdie, which was I think in Aberdeenshire, with attractive wooded grounds, and a large stable block which housed one, rather bad-tempered, piebald pony. I looked after this pony, fed it, groomed it, rode it and now and again put it in the trap and went down to the village but it was not a very harmonious relationship. It hated Freuchie and was always trying to kick him.

There was a big billiard room and this was where I learned to play billiards. I was taught by Mr Horne who, like the piebald pony, went with the house but he was better tempered. He was a kind of general handyman, looked after the grounds and cleaned the men's shoes. If there were any practical problem about the house, Mr Horne would sort it out He was a bit of a joker as well, there were swing doors into the kitchen quarters and whenever we met there, he would hold one open for me to go through before him and say "age before beauty". I didn't know what he was on about. "He's a cheeky one that," Bella said about him. I became very engrossed in billiards and practised away happily by myself. When grown-ups came wanting to play a game I was very put out unless I was allowed to chalk their cues. I remember that Francis had quite a few of his Oxford friends to stay including Thurstan Irvine. Tur, as he was known as, married Bud several years later. I don't know if any spark was struck that summer but I do remember she and I commenting on the fact that Tur wore khaki shorts rather than the more usual 'Oxford bags' which were grey flannel baggy long trousers. He sometimes carried a sheath knife and could be seen early in the morning before breakfast stalking round the lawn and flipping it at any mole that might appear or the unwary rabbit. As far as I know he never hit anything. He and Francis went on a couple of fishing holidays together to Norway. Tur and my sister re-met during the war when she was still with the Atholls in Dunkeld and he was a curate nearby. They married when Elizabeth was in the W.R.N.S., from which she got her discharge after breaking her leg and a serious illness caused by a clot on her lung. I was in Cairo and so sadly I was unable to be at their wedding. Also I did not know how ill Bud had been until after I got home.

The holiday, and I think it was the last summer holiday we spent in the Highlands, that I still remember very clearly was the joint holiday we had with the Colvins on the island of Mull. It was a biggish house, a few miles from Tobermory, called Lindhu and we could see the sea. It had extensive untamed grounds and a small formal rose garden and it was not unusual to see deer early in the morning or late evening. My aunt Sophie and uncle Ian and my cousin Anne and their fox terrier Jerry motored up from Wimbledon and they arrived after we were installed. Anne was two years older than me and like me she was the youngest in her family with three elder brothers. Only one visited us that summer, Duncan, the eldest, who I thought was lovely because he paid me some attention which understandably my own brother did not.

I thought Anne was very lucky, Duncan was several years older than Francis and worked in the woollen trade in the Midlands. He taught me to drive his car in an empty field. Of the other two, George was in the Royal Navy and that summer was cruising in the China Sea, he became a submarine commander and his submarine was torpedoed in the Mediterranean during the war. I was told that while sitting on the ocean's floor he used to do tapestry work to pass the time and keep his nerves calm. The youngest, Ian, was a journalist like his father, it was through him that my parents later on were put in touch with the von Varnbüler family in Stuttgart. Uncle Ian was editor of the *Morning Post*.

It was to the Colvins I went for breakfast at the start of each term when I was at Sherborne School. I would get off the night train from Edinburgh and take a taxi out to Wimbledon and they would be at breakfast when I arrived in their solid red brick house on the The Ridgeway. Uncle Ian would be breakfasting wearing a silk dressing gown. I thought that was very bohemian, my father was always dressed and shaved for breakfast! Then after lunch, Aunt Sophie took me to Waterloo Station and put me on the school train. I hated Waterloo with all those girls milling around wearing green coats and skirts and fawn, felt paddy hats. And of course it was to Aunt Sophie that Rosemary and I turned after we had been bombed out, by which time she was widowed and had moved to Lingfield Road.

But it was a great summer that at Lindhu, the weather was particularly good and there were lots of excursions and picnics and walks. Freuchie and Jerry hated each other and I spent a lot of time keeping the peace between them. The bathroom at Lindhu was quite unusual, it was a big room in the middle of which was a big, oval iron bath, the lavatory was up three steps on a dais and had a mahogany lavatory seat so it was well named the throne room. Every evening when I had my bath I took the dogs upstairs and put one in each corner of the bathroom and dared them to move while I was having my bath. It wasn't until I had dried myself and gathered up my things that I lifted my ban and they would scramble together through the open door, growling, and race down the stairs. But they never actually had a fight.

There was a Highland pony, a plump docile chestnut which Anne and I had fun with riding around the place. But we got into trouble with its owner who was the daughter of our landlord because we cut its mane. We thought it looked rather ragged so we straightened it out with a pair of cutting out scissors, she was very cross. Anne, who was to become a very interesting painter, spent a lot of time drawing and I remember one wet Sunday she shut herself into the so-called library, and emerged at lunchtime with an intricate painting of a Snakewoman. We had the usual visit from Aunt Totty but accompanied this summer by Uncle Hugh who had retired from his job as medical officer with the Madras-Bombay railway. Brother and sister now lived together in the Edinburgh flat.

Some fifty years later, in 1990, Bud and I returned to Lindhu. It was now an hotel and we booked in for a weekend. It was very strange going back. The grounds and the lower rooms were still familiar and the rose garden unchanged but upstairs there had been various alterations and the throne room had given way to small, boring modern bathrooms. We took along an album of our father's photographs which the hotel staff were interested in looking at. I love the island of Mull and when I visited again felt I could have lived there perhaps, but I love Mallorca more. They have similarities despite their geographical differences and they both suffer from too many tourists.

Well, Alex, I think I must end this rather rambling letter on my childhood holidays but just to finish I should tell you that when I was sixteen I went with my parents on a cruise to the Canary Islands, my first contact with 'abroad'.

Looking forward to seeing you very soon,
   Lots of love
      from g'ma
         Veronica

Dearest Stephanie

In another two months you will have finished your course and be qualified. I bet you will be glad when it is over. You say that you will be looking for a job within a twenty-mile radius of home. I wonder what you will feel returning to Wiltshire after all those years teaching English in different countries? Now you will be teaching Spanish and French to British children.

Returning is often a mixed experience. I have had several 'returnings' in my life: the devastating return from here to a trashed home in Newdigate, two years after your grandfather's death; the wonderful return from a Madrid hospital to St. Thomas's in London and innumerable returns to Scotland which I left as an adult. But I think the most difficult return was my return to Britain from overseas during the war, in June 1944.

Work was beginning to dry up in Conversano, in Italy. Quite often we did not have enough to do. The Germans were being chased up Italy, everyone was talking about the second front. D Day was imminent and personnel were required elsewhere. Rosemary and I were informed that we had been posted back to England, to Bletchley Park, the great parent organisation of all those scattered wireless listening posts. That strangely kind fate which had allowed Tom and me to be together for nearly two and a half years had another card up its sleeve – Tom was also posted home, not of course to Bletchley, but to some as yet to be assigned post. There were several others who were going as well. It seemed as if 276 Wing might be breaking up.

We were all transported with our baggage (and mine included a barrel of wine) to Naples, to await the boat home. The male officers went to a transit camp in a villa on the outskirts of Naples and Rosemary and I were housed in a deserted block of flats in the centre of town. It was not a large block, not more than ten flats, but they were all empty and open, where the occupants had gone we had no idea. Anyway we explored them all and decided in which one we would set up our camp beds and make our temporary home. The flat had a bathroom but obviously no hot water, luckily it was summer, and warm. It was not exactly a home from home. The flat doors apparently had no keys but the military fixed us a new lock on the front door so we were able to lock up at night and when we went out. For our food we went to a Mess for officers in transit, a few streets away. In all, I think the stay in Naples lasted two or three weeks.

Tom and I met most days. We climbed Vesuvius, the still warm larva, which the volcano had spewed out when it erupted some months previously, singeing the soles of our shoes. We remembered how Conversano had spent a day in near darkness the day Vesuvius erupted, although nearly 100 miles away. We visited Pompei and Herculaneum and in the evening went several times to the opera. Life in Conversano had been very much country life so it was exciting to be in a city again and one that was quite buzzing despite the war. Naples was full of foreign forces, GIs being predominant.

We had to report every morning at 10 a.m. for news of our boat, after which we were free to do as we wished. We took the bus to Sorrento and enjoyed ourselves poking about this deserted and closed-up resort, peering through the padlocked iron gates of shut-up villas, then took ourselves off to the empty beach where we watched and chatted to fishermen and ate our picnic. News came through that the Germans had retreated north, out of Rome. Tom and I were tempted to try and get there. There was still no news of the boat and once it arrived there would probably still be two or three days before we embarked. It was a risk and we would have got into serious trouble if things had gone wrong. Rosemary said she would do her best to cover up for us if anyone asked awkward questions at the reporting depot.

Tom slept that night in our flat and at 6.30 the next morning we got up and made our way on foot and by tram to the outskirts of Naples, aiming for the road that led north, the famous Highway 17, where we intended to hitch a lift. Our luck was in. Within minutes almost, an American army lorry stopped for us; they were going straight through to Rome so we hopped in the back and were on our way.

For the first forty or fifty miles the countryside looked green and serene and as if the war had never touched them, country people were working in the fields. Then the scenery changed dramatically as we drove into the area of the recent fighting By the roadside were the remains of charred tanks, upturned vehicles and smashed guns. It seemed as if not even the smallest cottage had escaped the blast of war. At intervals along the road there were notices saying how many feet from the verge had been swept for mines. We now came across refugees trudging in both directions, some hopefully trying to thumb a lift, but most seemed resigned to walking. As we passed the Pontine Marshes we could see that there had been heavy flooding which had made most homes uninhabitable – natural disaster vying with the horrors of war. The sharp peaks of the tree covered Apeninne mountains looked down in aloof detachment on all these scenes of destruction and devastation.

It was early evening when we reached Rome and we suddenly panicked that we might have to show some permit of entry, which we didn't have. But all was well, we drove straight into the centre of Rome and the Americans set us down in the Corso Umberto. It was an exciting moment. American and Italian flags draped the buildings and the streets were full of exhausted, battle stained GIs. Our first aim was to find a room for the night. Most hotels had been commandeered by the Americans and as yet no canteens or hostels had been set up for other Allied forces. But we did find a room in a big, empty luxury hotel. It was under Swiss management and had not been commandeered by the Americans nor, apparently, by the Germans. They had no food and were very apologetic that they could not feed us but told us where we could find an open restaurant nearby. There, we had a very basic meal and there was no wine. It was said that the Germans or the *tedeschi* as the Italians call them, had taken all the wine in Rome with them when they left.

The next morning we sallied forth to have a look at some of the sights. Rome was undamaged and the adults and children looked well dressed and not as underfed as so many of their compatriots in other parts of the country. There were a few more Allied troops about and at one of the busy intersections a British MP (military police) was on point duty. The GIs were gazing into shop windows full of luxury goods costing the earth, it was the basic goods of life that were in short supply. The great happening of our day was when we were exploring the Colosseum in the company of dozens of GIs. We heard in the distance the sound of pipes and it got louder and louder until a contingent of the Seaforth Highlanders swung into the Colosseum. Once there, they danced for about half an hour – a series of highland flings, sword dances and other Scottish dances.

It stirred even my rather sluggish Scottish blood, now somewhat thinned after so long in hot countries! Tom took many photographs and later on the series was published in *Picture Post* and was really the kick start to his photographic career. Early that evening we got ourselves to the southern outskirts of Rome to hitch our way back. We had a long wait, there was very little traffic and it was quite dark when eventually we were picked up. Once again it was the Americans and we were very lucky that they were going straight to Naples. It was a military car and a much more comfortable ride. So that has been my only visit to Rome, I never went back in peacetime.

We arrived back in Naples around breakfast time. We had not been missed and no awkward questions had been asked, there was still no news of the boat. But of course it did eventually arrive and we embarked. Up until that moment I think I managed to repress what it actually signified – that Tom was going back to his wife Mary, that I was going to pick up the tab, in other words to come to terms with a bleak and uncertain future. I barely saw Tom on the voyage home, partly because the male officers lived in a different part of the boat (Rosemary and I lived with a large contingent of Service wives from Malta who were being taken to England) and partly because I think Tom needed to put himself into emotional quarantine before his arrival in the UK.

When we docked at Gourock, the port from which I had sailed two and a half years previously, I caught a glimpse of him in a motor launch among others being ferried ashore – and that was it. Rosemary and I were given instructions to report to RAF Headquarters in Ad Astral House in London. I knew I should have taken the same train as Rosemary to London but Glasgow was a short train journey from Edinburgh and after all this time I wanted to see my parents before travelling south.

So Rosemary and I parted company and I went through to Edinburgh. My parents did know I was on my way back but they had no idea when to expect me so when I walked into 12 Albert Terrace it was a great surprise. My mother wasn't there, she had gone to Aberdeen to visit Francis at the T.B. Sanatorium. But my father and Bud were at home. We sent my mother a telegram and she rang me up from a call box that evening. Bella rustled up a tasty supper, I had a hot bath and a comfortable night in my own bed. It was so strange to be at home again, it didn't feel quite real – I missed the presence of my little dog, Freuchie. Elizabeth was still living at home because she and Tur had nowhere to live and she was expecting her first baby, Rosemary, in about a month's time. It wasn't until Tur became a curate in Dunfermline that they got their first home.

The next morning I caught the London train and when the following day I reported to Ad Astral House in Kingsway, I was in deep trouble. I had to report to a top brass WAAF officer. Queen Bees we used to call them. First of all I was improperly dressed. Overseas we were allowed to wear forage caps and somewhere along the way I had lost my peaked cap and so was still wearing what was nicknamed a fore and aft. As I stood rigidly to attention before her imposing desk, Madame looked me up and down disdainfully and asked – "What is that thing you are wearing on your head?" She knew perfectly well, however I explained that I had lost my proper cap and that overseas we wore forage caps. I was told to go and buy a 'proper' cap immediately and come and see her again when I was properly dressed. So I went off to find the nearest military outfitter where I could buy myself a new cap and returned in the afternoon. This time I was told my hair was too long and to get it cut and finally of course I was ticked off for being late in reporting. It cut no ice when I told her that I had gone briefly to see my parents who I hadn't seen for two and a half years. That was what my disembarkation leave was for I was told. Finally my welcome home came to an end and I left Ad Astral House with a leave chit for two weeks and a return rail warrant to Edinburgh.

London was grey and shabby and dismal, even in the summer sunshine and many of the faces of the passers-by were lacking in animation and energy. Life ground on without much to lighten the daily routine. Buzz bombs were now a feature of life in London and added to the uncertainty and sense of danger. Certainly in the women's services, we who had been overseas were looked upon as having 'escaped' and in a sense I suppose we had, attitudes overseas were more relaxed and informal, military 'bull' was kept to a minimum.

Tom's return to Mary was disastrous – hellish for him, tragic for Mary. I suppose, in a way it was predictable and it was naïve to have thought otherwise. When Tom had been posted to Egypt, he and Mary had been married for just over six months. He and I had been together for two and a half years and had shared so many experiences. He solved his immediate

196

problem by asking for another overseas posting. He found the situation untenable and I think wanted to deal with it from a distance. 'A plague on both their houses' attitude maybe. Anyway he was posted to Normandy and subsequently to Antwerp.

At the end of my disembarkation leave I went south again, to Bletchley and for the first few weeks Rosemary and I were billeted in a pub in Newport Pagnell. Tom left for Normandy shortly afterwards and before he went we met in London and stayed with his friend Philip Thornton in Chelsea. I got letters from Nomandy, from a cider apple orchard where his unit was housed in tents. Bletchley was my last posting of the war and I have to say I was pretty miserable there. Rosemary and I saw very little of one another, mainly because we worked in different Huts and I was on shift work. We were moved out of our pub billet and Rosemary went to share a house with some of her colleagues where she was very happy.

I was billeted in a little town about twenty minutes bus ride away from Bletchley. It was a street of uninspiring red brick terraced houses. I had a room on the ground floor at the front of the house, the sitting room really. I had to use my camp bed as there was no other. This billet was somewhat reminiscent of the billet in Dalmeny but cleaner. The WC was in the yard and my landlady brought me hot water every day to wash in my room. There was no bathroom. She was perfectly civil as was her family but not friendly and I had a surfeit of plums and custard for my pudding! A coach ferried all of us who lived around, to Bletchley and brought us back.

Apart from being physically separated, Rosemary and I were on very different personal trajectories. She had been definitively separated from her army lover since we left Egypt and was intent in shaping her life's future. I was living in a sort of vacuum of uncertainty, unsure of my future and anxious for Tom's safety in the new theatre of war. Rosemary remained in the WAAF after the end of the war in Europe and she was sent to Washington to work on Japanese intelligence.

Bletchley Park was a large, not very beautiful Victorian mansion, standing in its own grounds and overlooking a small lake. Wherever there was space, prefabricated huts had been put up and in those we worked. Where I worked, I was the only non-civilian which made me feel rather the odd one out. I don't mean they were unfriendly, they were not and my boss was a particularly nice man, but they had all been a unit for such a long time that it seemed like gate crashing a family. I think there were about twelve of us altogether and we worked two eight-hour shifts. It was a pretty dreary existence, being endlessly bussed between my billet and BP, as we called it, with nothing much in the way of distraction, apart from my little wireless and reading. Winter was coming on so the weather was also dreary. Where was all that colour, sound, and light? Daily I scanned the letter rack for possible communications from Tom.

By now Hitler's second secret weapon was in operation, the V2 which followed on his other guided missile, the V1 or buzz bomb. It was named thus because it made a puttering noise as it went through the air and then there was about 10 seconds silence before the explosion. The V2 was much more lethal and sinister, it was completely silent and the first one knew of it was the (much bigger) explosion. The V2 was being launched against London and also Antwerp where Tom now was. On my 48-hours pass I would sometimes go up to London and stay either with my aunt Sophie in Wimbledon or with Philip Thornton and his wife and we would go to the theatre or a film. But the ever present threat of the V2s made London not very attractive.

Eventually Mary agreed to divorce Tom and it was she who sent me the telegram, first informing me that Tom had been bombed, then a few days later a second telegram telling me where he had been sent to in England. Mary was a very generous spirited person and when Tom died in 1959 she wrote to me and we corresponded over a short period of time. It has always been a cause of regret to me that we lost touch. When the V2 struck, Tom was in the Mess, having a drink. It was just before lunch so there were a lot of men there. The entire building was razed to the ground and Tom was buried under the debris for twelve hours. He was in a particularly uncomfortable position with his right arm doubled beneath him but his left arm was free and he managed to get at the policeman's whistle which he always carried in his breast pocket with just such an emergency in mind. He kept on blowing it at intervals for so long as he had the energy and when they dug him out they said it was the whistle that had alerted them. They operated on his head to remove pieces of glass from his brain and for the rest of his life he had a small circular hole in his skull and he was told not to play football.

Then they sent him back home to hospital at RAF Wroughton, near Swindon. It was just before Christmas, I got a 48-hour pass and travelled up to London where I spent the night in an hotel near Russell Square. It appeared to be full of rather drunken naval personnel, so I locked my bedroom door and tried to sleep. But what with the ancient plumbing and the noise of the revellers it was rather difficult. Next morning it was snowing and I got on a slow (very slow) train to Swindon. It was perishingly cold and of course no trains were heated in the war. Eventually it arrived in Swindon which was then a very dreary railway terminus town. I found a bus that went to Wroughton which was also very slow because not only was it snowing but it had become foggy as well. The bus dropped me off at the hospital. I was directed to the ward where Tom was and then I saw him, propped up against the pillows, with his shaven head, looking a ghost of his former self. At first we just sat and held hands without speaking. I visited again the following morning and Tom was able to tell me more about what had happened to him. Apparently only he and one other man had been rescued alive from the ruins of the building.

I had to leave Wroughton at midday in order to be back in time to go on duty the next morning I felt miserable leaving Tom but he was alive, safe and being looked after. I collected my things from the cottage in the village where I had spent the night. I had had to break the ice on the ewer of water in my room in the morning before I could clean my teeth ! But it had stopped snowing although the ground was icy. It is so weird, Steph, when I now stay with your Mum and Dad in Swindon and sometimes we drive up through Wroughton to Barbery Castle to go for a walk on the Downs. Of course RAF Wroughton has gone, but I peer at the houses as we drive past and try to identify the cottage where I stayed that night, but they're all so gentrified and smart now, it doesn't look the same place that I remember.

With Tom back in the UK and the divorce proceedings about to be set in motion, Bletchley Park did not seem quite so dire. But nevertheless I was not in a good state. I felt excruciatingly tired the whole time and endlessly anxious. It was my job when on the midnight shift (because my coach left later than the civilian girls') to lock up the safes, the card indexes and finally the doors, (there were two) of the Hut and then deliver the keys to the appropriate place. When I got back to my billet about 1 a.m. and was lying on my not very comfortable camp bed, I would worry as to whether I had really locked this or that up and sleep came late.

I decided to go to the M.O. thinking he might prescribe a tonic. Instead of which he sent me to hospital, and in Blackpool of all places! I said I didn't want to go and he said too bad, you need a rest. The hospital was a little way out of Blackpool and had been an hotel and had a golf course, it was entirely RAF. The first night at supper a Flight Lieutenant, sitting next to me, asked "Which floor are you on?" When I told him the second floor where I had been assigned a room, he replied "Oh, the loony floor." Thanks very much, I thought and determined to investigate this after supper. True enough, the hospital was organised in floors, the ground floor was surgical, the third (top) floor was medical and the second floor was psychiatric.

As I became acquainted with my fellow patients on the 'loony floor', I learned about their problems. There were several pilots suffering from 'battle fatigue', others who hallucinated and there was another WAAF who had been in a very bad car accident and who had been moved up from the surgical floor once her physical injuries had healed, she had terrible nightmares and could not sleep. We became quite good friends although it did not outlast our hospital stay. I felt a bit of a malingerer but to the hospital staff I was just another patient. At bedtime we had to line up for our sleeping pill, known as the blue bomb. I said I did not need it but was told that everyone in psychiatric had to take a sleeping pill. I got adept at not swallowing it and then spat it out down the loo. Our psychiatrist was a very good looking Wing Commander, very aware of it and full of himself. I saw him twice a week and what we talked about I cannot now remember. I only remember that I did not like him. But it did occur to me that if I played my cards right I might be able to get my discharge.

Tom was about four weeks in Wroughton Hospital and then he was discharged on sick leave and went home to his parents in Iver, near Slough. He now had a wound stripe on his uniform. Although he was a lot stronger he was still quite fragile and jumpy. The impending divorce came as a great shock to his parents who were very fond of Mary, I was an unknown quantity. Tom had written to his brother Wilfred with the idea that he should break the news gently to his parents but unfortunately Wilfred read out the entire letter at breakfast so they received it full in the face.

They were always very kind to me and I think in the fullness of time became quite fond of me. Tom was, I think, his mother's favourite, but he quite often had words with his dad. The divorce was quite straightforward and problem free, Mary divorced Tom for adultery naming me as the co-respondent. Our friend Philip Thornton, who was a great dramatist, said that it would be all over the Scottish newspapers as my father was a known and respected Edinburgh citizen. He could not have been more wrong. It followed its appointed course anonymously and quietly.

After I had been about a week at Blackpool, I noticed I was feeling so much better. The cessation of responsibility had lifted my feelings of exhaustion and anxiety and I thought that any moment they would send me back to Bletchley. I was not keen on the idea. I had developed a strong aversion to being in the Forces. It had been five and a half years and I wanted OUT. I wanted to be mistress of my own life again, to retrieve my autonomy. When he felt stronger Tom came to Blackpool for a couple of days and it was so wonderful to be together again that my urge to get out was strengthened. I kept my feelings of improvement to myself and I do not now remember what I said to the Wing Commander but he sent me home on sick leave with a medical discharge pending. This was sometime around February 1945 and towards the end of March my demob papers came through. I celebrated VE Day in May as a civilian, and for me it was a double celebration.

So, Steph, that was my return to Britain. Best of luck with your job search and I do hope you find a school in a place where you want to be, but you may have to be flexible.

Lots of love, see you soon, I hope,
your loving g'ma
Veronica

Dearest Jason

It was great to see you and Daniela and little Max in Fornalutx last week. Now you will be on the island in the Adriatic where Daniela's family came from, so have a lovely holiday in Croatia and a safe return to Chicago – I expect Max will be walking by then.

I have now been a week in Pedruscada which you know well from your holidays here as a child. What I think you don't know is how this part of Mallorca became so knitted into our lives, as well as Fornalutx which is my home. Early in 1960, after we had got through Christmas which I had dreaded, I began to have thoughts about finding somewhere on the sea where we could go for the summer holidays. I know Fornalutx is *near* the sea but I wanted to be *by* the sea so we didn't have to drive anywhere in the van. We actually spent that Christmas day (1959) with the Graves in their house in Deià, and with other children around it was less awful than I had feared. When I went to bed that night I found a little pencilled note from Cordelia and Fi. It was written by Cordelia and thanked me for a Christmas *as good as ever but it would have been nicer if Daddy had been there.* It was the poignant understatement that pierced my heart and that night I cried myself to sleep.

Gradually the germ of this idea began to form a specific picture in my mind. Somewhere right on the sea where the children could roam freely. The tourist development of the Mallorcan coast was only just beginning but even so I wanted to avoid anywhere that smacked of a tourist resort, so I thought the best thing to do was to take the van and drive around and have a look. The children were by now well integrated in the village so I had no qualms about leaving them with Magdalena to look after them. I went off for a day or maybe it was two days, I can't now remember, but I think I may have stopped off the night in some small pension.

The roads in Mallorca at the beginning of the sixties were still nearly all dirt roads. The only tarmac roads were from Palma to Pollença and Palma to Alcudia and of course the road over the *coll* to Sòller from Palma. From Fornalutx, the American road, as it was called, because it was built with American money and which tunnelled through the mountain and now gives access to the north of the island, was still not finished. So driving around in a not very well sprung Ford van was quite a tiring business.

Anyway, I set off on my quest on a bright February morning. I avoided the coast round Palma, I knew that was not what I was looking for, and started to work my way up the east coast. There were lots of pretty bays and beaches and small villages which by today's standards were quite unspoilt, but there was not one that especially grabbed me. As I proceeded further north the road left the coast and came inland. I reached Capdepera which you may remember is built on a hill. I drove through it and came down towards the sea again on a dirt road with dark pine woods on either side. At the bottom of this road there was a huddle of cottages facing the sea. I parked the van on the coastal track and got out to have a better look.

As I took in the small rocky bay and the five or six whitewashed cottages with brightly painted shutters, literally yards from the sea, I knew that this was what I had been looking for – this was it. But the question was whether any of those cottages were for rent. There was no one about and the cottages were all shut up so I thought I would make my way into Cala Ratjada to see if I could get any information. At the next bay, Son Moll, there was a little beach shop and I went in there. "Oh yes," said the man, "one of the cottages is mine and I'd be happy to rent it." I arranged to meet him there in an hour's time.

Meanwhile I went back to the bay and sat down on the jetty which jutted quite far out into the sea, and scrutinised the little houses. They didn't look that Mallorcan, whitewashed and every house with different coloured shutters and doors, more like something you would expect to find in – say, Greece. Very unlike the solid stone houses in Fornalutx. They had double wooden doors, boat house doors, as these cottages had been fishermen's cottages and the jetty a small working fishermen's port. I sat speculating which one might belong to the beach shop owner. There was one very narrow one, set back a little and taller than the others. It had pale blue shutters and doors and rather took my fancy and indeed that was the one the man unlocked when he finally turned up. It was on three floors, the boat house on the ground floor, with a drop lavatory in a dark cupboard at the back, then a good sized room on the first floor with door sized shutters overlooking the sea and in a small room at the back was a very primitive Mallorcan kitchen with two charcoal burners and a vent which was open to the sky. Then up another narrow staircase to the top floor which had a small square room opening on to a little balcony. In this room was a double bed with sagging springs and a lumpy mattress and by the window a worm-eaten table with a rickety chair. The room was entered from a landing almost as big as the room. The interior of the cottage had been newly whitewashed and even in its primitive state it charmed me. The stretch of incredible blue and turquoise sea seen from the windows and the sound of the lapping water were irresistible. The owner proudly informed me that it was wired for electric light but had not yet been connected and I would have to use oil lamps and candles. So did I want to rent it? As it stood, he wasn't supplying any fancy comforts. Of course the answer was yes. He agreed to let it to me for six months from April and the amount was the then equivalent of fifty pounds.

It turned out to be a good decision. It did not take me long to figure out what was needed to make the place habitable. I suppose I must have some residual pioneering spirit in me because I always seem more attracted to the primitive and simple rather than the smart and sophisticated. I think it was the Russian writer Pushkin who said – 'the greatest luxury in life is selective simplicity'. Well, our little boathouse (Blue Shutters we called it) was simplicity unlimited. I rigged up a perfectly serviceable kitchen in the boat house, a big trestle table down the middle with a wooden bench on either side, I cooked on a two-ring camping gas stove on a plastic table against the wall and the 'sink' consisted of a bowl and a bucket. On the walls I hung several of the old style Mallorcan oil lamps. Those consisted of small, square, shallow iron containers which were filled with oil and into which were put lengths of wick which supped up the oil and when lit, burned away slowly, giving a faint soft light. Where we needed a stronger light we used candles. In our primitive lavatory I installed 'electric light' in the shape of a powerful torch hung on a nail. Bedding was brought from home and I bought four cheap foam mattresses. I made do with the lumpy wool one and the creaking spring bed in what was to become my room. An important piece of equipment was the big fly curtain which I had made to measure to hang across the downstairs doorway. The doors stood wide open all day and it helped to soften the sun's rays in the morning and deter unwelcome insects which mercifully were few. The middle room where the boys slept had the most space and we used it to keep the children's clothes which were minimal, books and non-beach toys. The little room off it, which appeared to be a kitchen, I turned into a wash room. Cordelia and Fiona slept on the landing outside my room.

That summer of 1960 had a magical sense of release about it, not much routine and no school. It was just seven months since Tom left us and I think all of us to a certain extent had been confined in the strait jacket of mourning. Beneath our 'normal' life, which I had tried to re-establish as soon as possible, we each individually were trying to come to terms with our devastating loss. I think that mourning is a solitary business and that's probably why certain cultures have stylised communal mourning rites, but it's not part of Western culture. Of all the children Tom Simon was the most vocal in his distress and disorientation, Cordelia surrounded herself with impenetrable reserve and Martin used the escape route of realism – this is what has happened and you have to get used to it. Fiona was too young to understand what it was all about and as she was little, I could pick her up and cuddle her without words which gave me some comfort.

So that summer in Pedruscada we were somewhere which had no connection with our immediate past, Tom had never been there and it was a fresh venture in our life without him. We had Mallorcan neighbours and there were other children with whom mine palled up and played with. Obviously most activities were sea based, they were all good swimmers like their father and unlike their mother. It was Fi and I who swam around near the jetty and all the children's efforts to get me to jump off it into the water were unavailing! The elder children would swim out to the *verde,* you know that green patch where the bed of the sea is sandy, nowadays it's three times as big as it was then. But they also played up in the pine woods where they had their *campo de flechas* – arrow camp. Those pine woods which now have all but disappeared and in their place neat suburban streets, villas, large and small, and apartments.

On Sundays we nearly always went to Cala Aguila, driving down the sandy road between pine trees which is now one long tourist strip of hotels, shops and apartment blocks. In those days there was a smattering of tourists but they were scarcely noticeable on the long stretch of white sand and the children loved the waves there which we didn't normally have at Sa Pedruscada. On the way home we would stop at the *fonda* in Cala Ratjada and eat a Sunday *paella* at long wooden tables and looking down on the turtles swimming around in their sea enclosures. The sea has now been pushed back and the area concreted for cars and pedestrians. The turtles are no more and the jellyfish proliferate. We would also go some evenings to

Cala Aguila and have an evening swim and a supper picnic. I had a tiny ceramic and iron grill which I fired with charcoal and on this we grilled sausages and sometimes fish which we ate on bread for our supper. By the evening the few tourists had departed and we had the entire beach to ourselves.

During that summer the owner of Blue Shutters wanted to sell it to me for the then equivalent of three hundred pounds. I didn't have three hundred pounds so then he suggested that I swap my van for it. He told me he had given the previous owner a motor bicycle. Quite apart from the illegality of it all I had no intention of parting with my van. Also I was not sure whether I wanted to assume responsibility for another property. But anyway he agreed to let me have the cottage the following year on the same terms.

I like to think that these long summer weeks had a healing effect on all of us. There were few demands, we had regular meals and a siesta about which I brooked no argument from the children, if they didn't sleep, at least they had to lie down and read and be quiet. I suppose I was a fairly controlling mother, more so because I was on my own than I would have been if I had not been a single parent. But with the responsibility of four children one could easily be overwhelmed.

They took turns in helping with small domestic chores. We had a well in one wall of the boat house, it wasn't very big and the water was used only for cooking and washing ourselves. Quite near us there was a lady who sold bottles of drinking water and lemonade and that was a fairly popular chore, to go and fetch the drinks. The most unpopular was throwing the *basura* (rubbish) into the sea, there was nowhere else for it to go. At least there was very little plastic, if any, then. Martin used to be particularly dilatory about it when it was his turn. Cordelia complained bitterly that I sent her off on her bicycle to get the rolls for breakfast past a house with two fierce dogs who rushed out and snapped at her ankles as she rode past.

Talking of dogs our little poodle, Tildy, got hit by a car fracturing one of his back legs and he had to be taken to the vet and the leg put in splints. But that was our only real drama.

Now and again we went back for a night to Fornalutx when we felt the need for a shower instead of a flannel down and to take back dirty clothes and collect clean ones. But they were fleeting visits and we were soon back by the sea. At night after the children were in bed, I would sit downstairs at the trestle table, lit by three or four candles and write to my family and friends or read and sometimes just sit and contemplate what lay in front of me. Little by little those solitary evenings helped me to reconstitute myself.

But of course all too soon the holidays were over and towards the end of September we returned home to Fornalutx to get ready for the autumn term. We were tanned and healthy from plenty of fresh air, sun and sea and we were pleased to be back in the mountains and in our own house again in the lovely valley of Sòller.

When, the following year, I got in touch with the owner again, he informed me that he had sold the cottage to a German couple who lived in Cala Ratjada and they were going to keep their boat there. But they had promised to honour his verbal agreement with me and would let me rent the cottage on the same terms until the end of September. I went to their house which was next door to the tennis courts and saw Margot, the wife, who gave me the key and I gave her the rent money. She was a very good looking, elegant woman, and friendly.

Our second summer (1961) at Sa Pedruscada passed very much in the same way as the previous one. We had one or two visitors and Beryl Graves came over with Tomàs and swept all the children off for the day to Cala Aguila with the object of freeing me so that I could get down finally to writing my article on home schooling, which I did at the worm-eaten table in my room. It was subsequently published in the *Daily Telegraph*. But this summer there was one big difference. At the beginning of September we returned to Fornalutx for a week. This was to get Cordelia and Tom Simon, packed and got ready to return to England to go to boarding school. The arrangements had all been set in motion for some time and Wilfred was to meet them and take them to family friends where they would be staying until their terms started. I remember one evening when I was down at the shop, catching a glimpse of Tom Simon sitting on the wall of the steps going up to the church. He was sitting with his legs hunched up and his face was dropped on his fists as he surveyed the evening's goings on in the square. I felt a stab in my heart as I realised his childhood was coming to an end. Their going was a terrible wrench, but for them it was traumatic. Looking back with hindsight and rather more experience, I'm horrified at what I did. But it was done with the best of intentions and luckily no lasting damage was done.

After they had gone, Martin, Fi and I went back to Sa Pedruscada. My sister Elizabeth came towards the end of the month to stay for a week. It was the first time I had seen her since Tom's death. I put her in my room and slept on Cordelia's mattress on the landing with Fi. We returned to Fornalutx at the end of September and that for many years was the end of Sa Pedruscada in my life. In March 1963 I returned to England with Martin and Fiona.

It was not until I retired, some twenty years later that Sa Pedruscada surfaced again in my life. That first summer of my retirement I left Fornalutx and went for two weeks riding in the Alpujarras, mountains in Andulacia. The following summer I had lots of visitors in Fornalutx but I had begun to think of that little cottage we had rented twenty years ago over the other side of the island and wonder what had happened to it. So I drove over on the considerably improved roads to take a look. As I drove down the road towards the sea through the pine woods, now liberally besprinkled with houses although not entirely urbanised as they are now, another twenty years on, I had the anxious feeling that the cottages might have disappeared and I would find some apartment block or hotel on the site. But no, miracles of miracles, there they still were, looking very spruced up and freshly painted, and sprouting TV aerials from the roofs.

I went in search of Margot and found her alone, living in a much reduced part of her former dwelling, most of which she had sold off to the tennis club. There was no sign of her husband and she seemed to have become alcohol dependant, but she was as good looking and charming as ever. She agreed to rent me her cottage for the months of July and August. That was in 1981 and you came with your mother for the first time. The cottage was certainly transformed and had all been modernised. On the top floor the small room had disappeared and the entire space was now one big room. It was both strange and familiar to be back again. We had more neighbours, all Mallorcan and the jetty sported two smart sets of steps, one lot going into the shallow part for the children and the other going into the deeper water.

The next year (1982) I drove back to Britain and spent the summer months in England and Scotland. But I was eager to get the cottage again for the summer of 1983, however I was to be disappointed. Margot had sold off the remainder of her property to the tennis club and was going to live in Pedruscada full time. So that was that. I asked around and one of the Pedruscada neighbours put me in touch with the owner of the flat about five minutes walk from Sa Pedruscada which you know so well and where I went for about the next twenty years. It served us well while Tom's children were growing up and they came more or less annually for three weeks. We were not able to step out of the door into the sea but we did have sight of it – remember – from the top terrace where the washing was hung, And that was a nice big balcony at the front, overlooking the derelict old house and its tangled garden, which subsequently metamorphosed into a small exclusive hotel with manicured grounds.

And now, with my ninetieth year creeping up on me, I'm back in our original cottage again in the summer. Margot did indeed take up permanent residence there for nearly fifteen years, summer and winter. In the winter of course she was entirely on her own because everyone else went back to Capdepera. As the years went by she became more and more reclusive, cutting herself off from her German friends and not seeming to want to have anything to do with anybody. Somebody did her shopping and she would open the door to take it in but otherwise it was closed. She did have a telephone installed and her Mallorcan neighbours kept an eye on her and rang up from time to time throughout the winter, but it must have been a very sad existence and in the end she became very ill and had to be moved to hospital where she subsequently died.

The cottage was inherited by her stepdaughter who lives in Palma. Eventually it underwent a second modernisation and now the kitchen is where I originally had it but a rather more sophisticated and modern version! However I still only have two rings to cook on, on the vitro ceramic top.

So Jason, that's the story of Sa Pedruscada and I hope I shall be able to enjoy it for a wee while yet.

Much love to you and Daniela and a kiss for Max,
G'ma Veronica

My Dearest Grandchildren
(including my great grandchildren)

I have tried in these letters to give you some idea of aspects of my life. Memory is a tricky thing. It can distort, exaggerate and confuse but I think basically what I have told is true. I haven't told you about my long and happy retirement here in Fornalutx, about my far flung journeys by boat, train and air to distant lands during my retirement because a lot of it you know already. Besides it would take another volume to write about.

Our lives are influenced not only by ourselves and others but by the historical time into which we are born and on which rung of the social ladder we find ourselves. I regard my own life as having been undeservedly privileged: I have never gone hungry, I have always felt loved, I've known neither wealth nor poverty and the early morning knock on the door has been the milkman and not the secret police. I suppose one thing my life has taught me is that quality is more important than quantity. I had a sadly short marriage but the quality of it has remained with me until now, rather like a deposit account in a bank, one can keep drawing on the interest.

You may well wonder why in all those years I never re-married. I'm not quite sure really. Certainly it was not a conscious decision. But in the early (and not so early) years after your grandad's death the task of caring for a young family by myself more than filled my days and left little room to contemplate anything else. And anyway who would have wanted to take on a family of four? Also I never consciously *looked* for another husband and whatever romantic prospects surfaced later in my life, they turned out to be totally unsuitable and blew up in my face or withered away.

213

Some people live several lives in their allotted life span but because no other family has entered the one Tom and I created, my life has felt very connected. Of course I have had my share of sorrow, frustration and unrealized ambition – I would have liked to have been a known writer – but this has been balanced out by so many positive and rewarding experiences that I can't feel hard done by. I started to write seriously in my retirement and although none of it except one novel has seen the light of day, it gave me great satisfaction to write and complete a work. It has been the engine of much of my life during my retirement.

Now in my advanced old age I am supposed to be wise and in a position to give advice to those much younger than myself. But I wonder. Your lives are lived in an increasingly consumerist and technologically dominated world. 'Things' are given great importance. In fact they have no real importance. Only people matter (and animals and trees and plants, everything that has life). Were I to proffer, tentatively, any advice, it would be this: centre yourselves on those you care about, give them your love, your interest, and be kind. Those who are unlovable, hate what they do and if necessary, condemn it, but do not lose compassion for the unlovable *person*. By all means enjoy the 'things' of this world, the big telly, smart clothes, the latest digital gadget, but ensure that if they were all thrown on the scrapheap it wouldn't make that much difference to the quality of your life.

I do not know why I am here or whether it has any purpose or importance, maybe it is entirely arbitrary. But I do know that I am very glad that I *am* here, that I have been given the gift of life and the health to enjoy it. But one must never be smug about one's own life, cast your eyes around you and remember that those in the direst circumstances could well be one of yourselves but for a quirk of fate.

I have lived my life by no clearly defined rules and principles, and certainly no conventional religious faith, but it has not been a chaotic muddle. Probably the best way to describe it is in the words of C.J. Jung in his *Memories, Dreams and Reflections*:

'There is nothing I am quite sure about. I have no definite convictions – not about anything, really. I know only that I was born and exist and it seems to me that I have been carried along. I exist on the foundation of something I do not know. In spite of all uncertainties, I feel a solidity underlying all existence and a continuity in my mode of being.'

My life is now approaching its inevitable end, but yours are in full flood. May they be fulfilled and rewarding so that when you come to be my age you will feel that same gratitude for the gift of life that has been yours. What more can I say? Except, that should there be a God, may he sprinkle you with his blessings.

Love to you all,
your loving grandmother
Veronica